WIN

INTERVIEW

A Complete Guide to Dominate Your Job Interview Thanks to Secret Skills and Techniques for Taking the Right Behavior and Giving Correct Answers

Brad James

Text Copyright©

Legal & Disclaimer

Upon using the contents and information contained in this book, you agree to hold harmless the Author from and against any damages, costs, and expenses, including any legal fees potentially resulting from the application of any of the information provided by this book. This disclaimer applies to any loss, damages or injury caused by the use and application, whether directly or indirectly, of any advice or information presented, whether for breach of contract, tort, negligence, personal injury, criminal intent, or under any other cause of action.

You agree to accept all risks of using the information presented inside this book.

You agree that by continuing to read this book, where appropriate and/or necessary, you shall consult a professional (including but not limited to your doctor, attorney, or financial advisor or such needed) before using any of the suggested remedies, techniques, or information in this book.

Table of Contents

Introduction

This book is aimed at providing you with the knowledge you need to excel in your job interviews. It will discuss how to get the interview you want, preparation for the interview, making a first impression, behavior during the interview, common mistakes and how to avoid them. Times have certainly changed, and so have the requirements and expectations of employers; what was acceptable or applicable a few years ago may not be so in the modern age. This also means that hiring practices are no longer the same.

You should now have a good understanding of how job interviews are conducted and how to prepare for it. After reading this book, you should be able to ace your next interview and land your dream job with great ease.

In an interview, everything from your appearance, your body language to your tone of voice matters. You may not be able to control everything but preparation will help you control most of it. The simple formula for success is preparation, alertness and the ability to think on your feet.

Work on your appearance and grooming because first impressions count a lot. Be comfortable and calm even when you feel anxious and nervous about the interview but not overconfident to the point of looking boastful and arrogant. Be generous on giving compliments. Ask if you must but be polite. Prove them how worthy you are as a future employee. Say thank you after the interview. When leaving, do not look like you are in a hurry. Do not make them feel like you want to end the interview as soon as possible.

Ultimately, when it comes to nailing a job interview, knowledge is power and preparation is key – that will never change. The question then becomes how can one adapt to changing hiring practices and ace a job interview in the current climate? What are the things one should know and how can one be best prepared? Read on to get answers.

Chapter 1: Understanding Job Interview

After sending out numerous job applications and patiently waiting, you've finally got the much-anticipated call to go for an interview with a potential employer. Having managed to get a job interview means you have surpassed countless other applicants vying for the job, and are among the shortlisted candidates deemed qualified to fill the position.

Job Interviews: Then vs. Now

In the not-so-distant past, people were oftentimes introduced to job openings through being referred by someone or by browsing the classified advertisements in newspapers. Competition was not as though, and if you were lucky enough to be referred by someone the employer knew and trusted, you were likely to already have an advantage over the other candidates.

However, when the Internet became the main outlet for recruitment and job searching in the new millennium, it changed the game. Job applicants began to have easier access to information on who was hiring, leading to a significantly higher response to job postings. Recruiters were then faced with the overwhelming task of sorting through hundreds, maybe even thousands, of applications and narrowing down potential candidates to a small handful. The selected few would then have to go through a tough interview process until the suitable candidate was found from among the hopefuls.

It is hardly a surprise that recruiters have changed their interviewing practices, and now take a tougher approach when screening for suitable candidates. Thus, job seekers now have additional criteria to fulfill in addition to simply stating their credentials, if they want to land that dream job in today's increasingly competitive environment.

What a Recruiter Wants

A job interview is a twofold process. On one hand, a potential employer will be gauging whether you have the capacity to competently fulfill the required role. The interview also allows for a company to form a well-rounded impression of whether a candidate has the personality and motivation to succeed in the particular industry for which they are interviewing. On the other hand, an interviewee has the opportunity to assess whether joining the organization is in line with their career goals, and is also given the chance to convince the hiring manager as to why they are the right fit for a job opening.

Perhaps the most baffling aspect of job hunting is figuring out exactly what recruiters are looking for. More importantly though, how can one get ahead of the pack to become that one outstanding candidate from many who actually lands the job?

The profile of an ideal employee differs from employer to employer. However, the basic tenets of having integrity, the drive to excel and the ability to learn quickly will generally get one noticed, especially if one has ambitions of climbing the corporate ladder. Even though there is no doubt that hard work, perseverance and diligence are essential qualities for success in any job, there are qualities outside of credentials and experience that will get the attention of employers – namely, attitude and mindset.

Businesses are facing various intense challenges in the current economy and market place. This increased competition has meant that companies now need to be lean and efficient. Thus, oftentimes they need employees who can do more than simply perform one particular function in the company. Favorable candidates are the ones who demonstrate creativity, commitment and passion to the job, showing that they are adaptable in a fast-paced working environment and are able to contribute to the business growth agenda in the industry for the long-run.

In summation, as a job seeker, your career survival and progression depends on how much you can contribute to an organization besides what is already specifically requested in the job description. The job interview is a window of opportunity in which you should be aiming to convince a potential employer that, not only can you fulfill the job requirements, but also you can bring more to the table than what is being requested.

Chapter 2: Company and Position

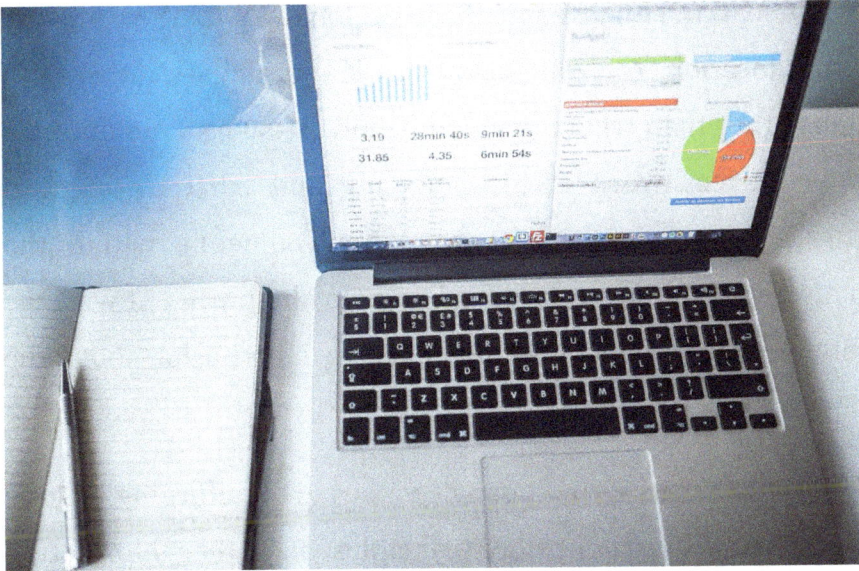

There are many reasons why researching the job is important before your job interview happens. Some of the reasons include:

- It is a tool to build knowledge about the company and make your interview process a more rewarding one

- It helps you get some detailed insights into the working of the company which will come in useful to you when you are answering some difficult questions posed during the job interview

- Researching will help you know if the job post and/or the company are legitimate in all respects.

Company Research

Start your search with a simple keyword lookup with the company name and location. You can begin to look at it and see if there are locations other than where you will be interviewing. Find out how many employees work at the company and what hierarchical structures there might be. If you know someone within the company, that could be a good lead and may help you out with the job interview. However, it is still ideal to know a lot about the company.

Come to understand the company's values and culture by looking at their mission statement, core principles, and other information about them. You can scour the Internet in search for these kinds of details. Think about their stock portfolio and how they are doing financially. Find out more about what this company stands for and what kind of work they are doing throughout the world.

Then, you need to think about this company and its values and consider how they align with your own. Note that you love the environment and want to do everything in your power to protect it. Here are the things you need to research on in preparation for your job interview:

Key Players

Don't just dig up information on the interviewer; you want to have some background on the key players in the company too. You can use this information to answer questions regarding inspirations and goals. Understanding the key player's journey through the company would be helpful in understanding the skills and experience required to make a powerful impact on the company. Sure, it sounds a bit too ambitious, but it is the ambition that gets you places!

Any Recent Events and News

Search for the company on Google. What all comes up? Is there any note-worthy information out there that you, as a prospective employee, need to really know about. Any mergers, downscaling, expansions, controversies that can help shape your answers better? Also, check Google News to read up on the latest scoop regarding the company. Knowledge of the recent events of the company and slipping them in through the interview will be a good indicator of your interest in the company. It will show that you have indeed prepared for the interview and are desirous of working for the company.

Company Culture

This is one of the core reasons you go through such a lengthy interviewing process, to begin with. Companies don't want to hire someone that would compromise on the culture. The culture of a company is extremely important in establishing a healthy and productive workflow. The companies know about it, and they don't want anyone compromising with it. Some companies like Zappos even conduct culture-fit interviews just to check if a prospect would fit into the company's vision and culture. They want someone that would adapt and embody that culture like their own. Be that person. A good way is to reach out to someone you know in the company to talk to you about the culture and employee relationships. Is the culture laid back and respectful? Is it about motivation and values? Understanding the culture can help set the tone for the interview, and you will be able to structure answers that resonate with the company's voice.

Know Their Competitors

You need to know about the market that you are working in. Who are the company's greatest competitors? Many times, hiring managers do bring this question, but you need to be prepared with the information at your arsenal. The objective of this information is not on how to tackle the competition but rather to know whether or not an applicant is aware of the industry, their products and services, and their market position in general.

Your Interviewer

In most cases, you will be told about who will be interviewing you. They may tell you a name or the designation, but beyond that, you could either depend on guesswork, or a little research. There may be just one person taking the interview or perhaps a team. Ask the Human Resources of the company for the names, titles, and roles of the interviewers when they call/e-mail you to set up an interview.

Hiring managers usually have an HR person contact the candidate in person to determine whether or not they are truly interested in the position offered and whether they are suitable to move forward. This screening interview is oftentimes conducted via a phone call or Skype.

This is also a good time to ask them about the hiring process, how many interviews and screenings do they do before the final verdict. Also, ask about who would be taking and attending each interview. HR recruiters are usually very accommodating about providing these details. All this information will help you map out the process and prepare accordingly.

Company research is an essential component of the overall job interview since it shows respect for the people that you desire to work with and to let them know that you have indeed done your homework. Even if you lack in skills and experience, your preparation and determination will more than make up for it. The recruiters will sure give preference to someone really wanting to learn and work with them than someone with a fancy resume but no drive.

Company Background

What is the company's vision and mission? What are its primary strengths? What does it specialize in? What are its plans in the future? What are its core values? Has it received accolades or distinctions from award-giving bodies? Find the answers to these questions and reflect on how you can help make things happen once you become a part of the company. Whether it's about providing the best healthcare in your city, or becoming the number one online advertising agency, it helps to know what the company's blueprint is all about.

Company Leadership.

Who will likely be your boss in case you get the job? Who are the company's top executives? How did they land their roles? What kind of leaders are they? Do you have the beliefs or qualities that you think they have? Is there anything admirable about them? When you research these types of information, you get to know how the company will likely treat its people because you get a glimpse of their leaders' personalities.

You can read executives' profiles on the company's website, and you can use these pieces of information during your interview. For instance, when asked why you decided to apply for a job in their organization, you can cite their leadership/management as one of your reasons and sufficiently discuss your answer.

Know About the Company's Products, Services and Clients

After all, the work you will be doing in the company will directly or indirectly affect the three components mentioned in this point: products, services and clients. Hence, knowing about these three elements with regard to your potential employer will help you customize your answers appropriately.

Additionally, if your skills and relevant experience include something that can have a positive impact on the company's relationship with one or more of its clients, then you can highlight these aspects during the interview process.

You can get information about the company's products and services from the website. You can find blogs and case studies and read and understand the company's way of doing things. Glassdoor.com is one of the better websites regarding these products, services, and clients. There are also very good previous employee reviews that quantify the likability of that employer.

Directions

If you are not sure about the exact location of the office where the interview will take place, do not hesitate to ask for directions. You do not want to be late on your job interview just because you got lost.

Job Description

This is important in preparing for your interview because all the things that you will emphasize during your interview have to be related to the job you are applying for. This will give you an area of focus so as not to waste time in preparing and also to prevent you from mentioning things that are irrelevant to your job.

Review the Job Posting

What's in a job posting you ask? Everything you would need to know about who the company is looking for. A good part of finding job interview success depends on applying to the right jobs. If you have been applying to pretty much any job available under where the sun shines for you, you are not very likely to find a lot of success. You will only be wasting a lot of valuable energy and would be resorting to template applications, cover letters, and interviews.

However, if you would only invest a small fraction of that time thoroughly reading and understanding a job description, you can go on to apply to the jobs most suited to your skills and thus have higher chances of success. Following are several things you should be focusing on when going through a job posting:

The Job Title

Almost every job posting has this, but not a lot of job-seekers take a good look at it. An editor's assistant and assistant editor might sound pretty similar, but there is a world of difference in their duties, qualifications, and skills. Be sure to dissect the job title word by word and truly understand what the said company is specifically looking for. You should be adding this job title in the subject line when sending in your resume and cover letter. There is a fair chance that the company is hiring for multiple jobs, and adding these specifications makes it easier for the recruiters to assess your application better. Not adding the job title could make it look like you are simply mass mailing your application and haven't really understood the requirements of the job.

Qualifications/Requirements/ Experience

This section explains in detail about what the company is really looking for. You would see details like the minimum education required, minimum prior experience, and other soft and hard skills needed for the job. It is not necessary to be able to tick all the boxes here, but you should feel that you are familiar with the skillset and understand the kind of employee the company is actually seeking. Focus more on the qualifications than the interpersonal skills. You may be a great 'team player,' 'motivator' and have great 'dedication,' but if you don't know how to code data or sketch a house plan, then there is a good reason you aren't a good fit for the job. Before they tell you the same after you focus so much of your time and energy on it, better you figure it out on your own.

Responsibilities

This bit describes what you are supposed to do at the job. Dissect it properly. Is it something that you believe you can handle or would enjoy doing? Do the responsibilities match with what you have done on your previous jobs? Don't be discouraged if you haven't been responsible for exactly the same tasks at your previous workplace. There may be little variations, and the company would be more than accommodating if you are otherwise a great fit. However, if the responsibilities don't make sense to you, then better stop reading further.

Experience

This bit outlines the level of experience required to apply for a job. Some may be looking for fresh graduates to train themselves while other jobs might require at least a number of years of experience. The salary and responsibilities vary for the same job depending on the level of experience. But if the job posting asks for three to five years of experience and you only have two years of experience, by all means, apply anyway. This requirement only means the company is not looking to train someone. And with two years of experience under your belt, you may just be the candidate they are looking for. Some job postings would specify what sort of experience they are specifically looking for. It may say something like 'three years of bookkeeping experience' or 'ten years of industry experience,' you better not ignore these. If they have bothered to be this specific, then they have a very good idea about the candidate they want to hire.

Research Tools

Hopefully you're beginning to see the importance of doing research before you attend your interview. Yes, it'll require some additional time and effort on your behalf, but the advantages you'll receive from doing so will absolutely pay off when you land the job.

Try a Casual Google Search

Before you apply or think about setting up an interview, do a quick Google search of the company or organization you are interested in. Take some time to browse their website if they have one. This step of research doesn't have to be intensive. Actually, it should only take you about 10-20 minutes. You simply want to know a little about your potential employer—what they value, what they do, and how they do it. The main idea is to get a general sense of whether or not your personal values and beliefs align with theirs.

The Website

This is the first place you need to visit. The company's website will have outlined everything you could possibly need to know about them. But don't just read about their background or map out the location, be thorough with your research. It will give you valuable information that you can use during your interview. Primarily, you should check the About Us section to read up about the history and the current practices of the company. The About Us section is a good place to know the background, mission, and goals of a company. Doing so would better help you understand the company's operations and values. Also, scour through the rest of the website to look for important keywords that will be indicative of what the company is actually looking for and the culture. For instance, if they use words like 'we are a family of...' then know that the culture is very friendly and warm. You can phrase your interview answers to resonate the same values that is, if you truly believe in them.

Social Media

Social media is a good place to check how the company wants to be portrayed to its prospective customers. How do they engage with them? What types of information do they share with them? All this information can really help shape your answers. Check all popular platforms of social media, including Facebook, Google+, Twitter, and Instagram. Companies that don't have an active social media presence or NO presence probably have a more traditional approach and might value the same from their candidates.

Read Their "About Us" or Company Statement

If everything went smoothly during your previous Google search and your values seem to mirror theirs, then it's time to spend a little more time learning about your potential employer. If a company or organization has a website, they generally also have an "About Us" or "Mission Statement" section as well. We strongly recommend taking some time to review these. Think of it like a cheat card—they provide brief but illuminating glimpses into the values, intentions, and aspirations of the company or organization. Referencing these elements during your interview demonstrate to your interviewer that you're interested, dedicated, and motivated. It also shows that you actually care.

Simply knowing what the company is about gives the interviewer an impression of how interested you are in working for them. In this modern age of technology, most companies have their own websites that you can visit and this is where you find out what they do, how they began, and who their looking for and this will definitely give you an edge over those lining up for that same position. This is also a way to help you get ready with regards to your qualifications so that you will be able to deliver the qualities you have that are relevant to what you are applying for.

Chapter 3: Exercise for Winning Interview

An interview is a very critical part of the screening process in order for you to get hired, therefore getting ready for that big day is just as essential. They say practice makes perfect and whether with a friend or in front of a mirror, it is important to PRACTICE. Have a list of questions to answer and practice answering them in the best possible way also while being aware of how you deliver them and your body language. Whether it's your walk, your posture, or you getting fired from a previous job, all things that you think need to be worked on whether big or small, has to be carefully handled before you even engage in the interview. It is just as important to remember not to sound like a robot just because you stuck to a script that you memorized word per word. Deliver your thoughts naturally and with sincerity. Try to create the general idea of your answers without having to put exact sentences together that were written down and memorized. Speak in the same manner you would like to be spoken to. Have someone listen to you and criticize you for your manners, tone, and other technicalities that you think are vital during the interview process.

Practice Answering Common Questions

Prepare yourself for answering the most common questions and topics that are discussed in interviews. These include: "Tell us about yourself," "Why you are interested in taking up this position in our company?" and "Why are you the best candidate?" Present a positive image of yourself and talk about how you can contribute to the organization. Remember to focus on what you can do for them, not what they can do for you. Prepare yourself for answering the most common questions and topics that are discussed in interviews. These include: "Tell us about yourself," "Why you are interested in taking up this position in our company?" and "Why are you the best candidate?" Present a positive image of yourself and talk about how you can contribute to the organization. Remember to focus on what you can do for them, not what they can do for you

Practice in front of the mirror, record your voice on your phone and listen to yourself, and do mock interviews with a friend.

Better yet, make a video recording of yourself while doing a mock interview. That way, you will become more conscious of your body language – specifically your eye contact and smile – and behavior.

You can then make adjustments to not only sound but also look confident, knowledgeable, dependable, and most of all, hirable.

Through practice, you can identify any mistakes you could potentially commit during the interview. There might even be bad habits that you did not know you had. Too many have stuttered nervously, blurted out curse words, sounded arrogant or even rude, or shared self-damaging personal information during an interview. Certainly, you do not want to be one of them. However, it is only through practice that you are able to identify your own mistakes and make the necessary corrections before the big day.

Calculate Travel Time

If it takes you 30 minutes to get to your destination, why not try to leave an hour before your interview? You want to avoid any chance of hitting heavy traffic and if you have a particularly long travel time ahead of you then put some added allowance on your travel time! Anticipate heavy traffic and other causes of delays. It is better to be safe than sorry.

Prepare Your Things Before Going to Bed

Whether or not you are that type of person who seems to be a little forgetful, try to accomplish tasks like organizing the things you have to bring for your big day and put them all in one place so that you don't misplace or forget that ball pen or that tie that you will be wearing for your job interview. Have a list of the things you need to bring check them one by one for you not to miss anything.

Your Skills, Experience and Qualifications In Relation To The Job You Are Applying For

It is very likely that you know all about your technical and soft skills, the experience you have gained, and how your qualifications helped you perform well in your professional life. Yet, it is imperative that you align these skills, experience, and qualifications in such a way that you can answer questions that are related to the job you have applied for.

Keeping these things ready will reduce any kind of last-minute pressure. Make a folder where you will keep all the necessary documents such as certificates, recommendation letters, **etc.** Keep the original as well as a couple of copies of each so that you can hand a full set of documents across the table if asked.

Eat Well, Sleep Well and Wake Up Early On the Day Of The Interview

Hunger and fatigue due to lack of sleep and stress are a deadly combination for panic. Be aware that such a situation can arise and counter it in by making sure you eat well, sleep early so that you get at least 6-7 hours of sleep the day before the interview, and set the alarm early. Do not get up late and increase the panic situation.

Try and go for a morning walk or jog to relax yourself. Have a healthy breakfast and get to the interview venue at least 15 minutes before time. Do not rush at the last minute. In the 15 minutes, try and gauge the environment. After this, simply relax with some deep breathing exercises.

What to Bring with You on the Interview Day?

Another good way to stay calm during the interview is by planning the things to take with you to the interview. This helps you to avoid any stress that could make you nervous.

Notepad and Pen: Carry these two tools because you may have to take some notes during the interview. If several candidates have the meeting on the same day as your interview day, and your interview time slot is not the first one, connect with those who do their interviews before you and ask them about the different things the interviewers asked then during the interview. They may spill a few beans you can take note of and use to your advantage during the interview.

Certificates: You should bring along evidence of your academic qualifications and previous jobs – bring along documents such as your exam certificates, previous work experience, letters, recommendation letters, performance awards, etc.

Photo IDs: You should have at least one photo ID – this can be your driving license or passport.

Money and Mobile Phone: You should have these two things with you to avoid and if need be, communicate any delays such as a flat tire or traffic jams that can keep you from reaching the interview on time.

List of References: You should have a list of references to give to your interviewer when he/she asks for it.

Water Bottle: Water helps you stay calm in situations where you become panicky. Also, sipping water right before a stressful situation such as an interview energizes you and improves your confidence. Therefore, ensure you carry a water bottle to every interview.

Anticipate Questions About Yourself and What the Interviewer Will Find in Your CV

While this book contains all of the most common interview questions, you won't get an explanation for every little detail. So, you must note down all the possible questions the interviewer will ask. That way, the interviewer will not catch you off-guard and you can provide an answer that might be crucial. Instead, be ready.

It will help to think of yourself in the interviewer's shoes as you analyze your own CV. You would be surprised by how easily these thought-provoking questions would pop into your head. For instance, you might even wonder why there is a big time gap between your jobs, or why you want to work as a secretary when your degree is clearly not related to it.

Compare Your Qualifications and Skills to the Job Requirement

Once you have all the knowledge you need about the organization you plan to work for, the next thing to do is compare your skills and qualifications to the job requirements. This way, you can understand and analyze the skills your interviewer may be seeking in the ideal candidate.

Comparing your qualifications, skills, and capabilities to that particular job requirement allow you to prepare an attractive "pitch" that makes the interviewer feel you are indeed the right candidate for the job. Here is how you can do that:

- To understand what skills and qualifications are necessary for a certain job you are applying for, the first thing you have to do is analyze the job description.

- You may not be aware of this exact term even though you used this approach when working in the HR department in your previous job posting. If you come across any such terms, look them up online so you can understand them.

- The third step is to recognize the particular pre-eminent qualification the particular company is interested in. Interviewers are looking for a certain skill/ability/talent in the different candidates in a bid to understand if they are competent enough to work in the firm. You, therefore, need to know the particular skill/talent your interviewer will be interested in so you can show him/her you are indeed qualified for that specific job.

- During the interview, you can tell the interviewer that since you have led various marketing campaigns in your previous job, you are qualified for this particular job.

Honing your CV, Cover letter and Resume Components

There is a high chance that you will want to adjust your CV, resume and cover letter several times after your research, and you really should do so. Keep in mind that your CV is a representation of who you are. It helps to look into the different types of resumes so that you can use a format that will put you in a good light, whatever your work and educational background may be.

Moreover, it helps to give the human resources department of the organization a call to ask how they would want you to present your paperwork. Once you have edited your CV, proofread it at least five times and then proofread it again the next day before printing it out. Also, make sure to have your portfolio neatly organized in a filing folder. That way, you can easily pull them any of them up if needed during the interview.

And since we are on the topic of working on your CV, it is important to note that your social media accounts (or anything that has your name on it online, for that matter) is also an extension of your CV. Any technologically-savvy interviewer would be wise enough to Google you or look you up on Facebook before or after an interview. Make sure to delete or set to private anything that would compromise your chances of getting hired. Nevertheless, be prepared to answer unusual questions about anything related to your online presence.

While resumes and cover letters, by themselves, are not sufficient to get you a job, they are integral parts of the job seeking process. Resumes and cover letters are the first impressions that you create. An organization filters resumes and cover letters to call candidates for job interviews. Believe it or not, the key to your resume is your achievements. Yes, it's important to note what you job you've done in the past, your education, as well as your skills and awards. However, your achievements are the ones that potential employers look at the most. Furthermore, providing **evidence** whether they may be **quantitated** or **qualitative** are highly smiled upon by potential employers.

It is imperative that you do a spell-check and a grammar-check on your resume and cover letter. Any kind of mistakes in basic communication mechanics is unforgivable. Moreover, your resume and cover letter will not even be looked at if these kinds of errors exist in them. So, spend some extra time on making sure your basic job application elements are free from spelling and grammatical errors.

Prepare Examples From Your Personal Experience

The best answer to any question during a job interview is an answer that is backed up with examples from your personal experience. This is especially true when you are asked questions about difficult or awkward situations, such as "What would you do if a client refuses to pay for the work?" or "What would you do if your subordinate didn't turn up for work and won't answer the phone?"

Think of Some Questions You Can Ask Your Interviewer

Show interviewers that you are interested by asking about what you read on the company's website. For example, you could ask them about the company's plans for the future or whom they see as their main competitors.

The Day Before the Interview: Refresh Your Memory

It's best to do items 1-5 above around 2-3 days before the interview. This gives all the new information time to settle in your mind. The day before the job interview, read all the notes that you took while preparing. Read the job description one more time and make sure that you understand every single word. Read the information that you noted about your interviewers.

Relax and Get Some Rest Before the Interview

After you finish the preparation, put all the materials and notes away and try not to think about the interview for at least 3-4 hours before going to sleep.

You've done all of the preparation already and now it is important to get enough rest and sleep in order to feel your best during the interview.

The best way to take your mind off the interview is to read a book or watch an interesting film. It is best not to drink any alcohol the evening before your interview as you will be less alert during the following day.

Create a Personal Folder

A personal folder is a collection of documents that pick up where your resume ends. It provides a more complete picture of you as a person than can fit on a resume. As an added benefit, it is nice to have the ability to look back at all of your past projects and accomplishments.

This folder can be a physical collection of documents or it can be saved in a digital format. If it is in digital form, make sure you take a device to the interview that can adequately display the content for the potential employer. You do not want to attempt to show them your achievements and projects on a phone screen.

Chapter 4: Clothing for a Winning Interview

Your looks matter, so dress to impress. What you wear makes the first impression to your interviewer. Of course, you should make sure you look professional and competent in order to set the right tone from the onset of the interview. However, on top of that, dressing professionally will add to your confidence. When you feel good about yourself, you are more likely to be in an extraordinary state of mind, positively impacting your performance.

In your preparation, make sure you know the company's culture to avoid being underdressed or overdressed. Based on your research, you should be familiar with their norms and expectations.

By taking a few precautions and dressing appropriately for the interview can let you interviewer know that you take your work and yourself seriously.

Dressing appropriately sets a vibe for you. It raises your confidence and sets a tone for the day. It starts off a mood, helps you focus and concentrate as it indicates that you respect standards of the workplace, and are willing to regulate.

Being presentable will help elevate your confidence levels and at the same time, set off the right tone with your interviewer. Workplace dress codes have become quite lenient in the past few years, but until you have truly identified with the place, it is better to keep it formal. Following are a few pointers to keep in mind:

Carefully consider the work environment. There are very few places you will get a job if you show up wearing something you'd wear to do work in the backyard.

As far as rules concerning dressing up for a job interview is concerned, nothing is carved in stone. No two companies are the same in what they consider as the acceptable dress code for an interview. So, your best option is to simply dress for success. It is not really that difficult in deciding what interview outfit to choose for that big day.

Here are some useful tips you can use on how to dress up for a job interview:

- Do some online sleuthing to find out what the dress code is in the company. Visit the company's website and see if there are photos or videos posted there. By watching the videos, you'd be able to get an idea on the over-all atmosphere prevailing in the company. Fashion yourself appropriately.

- Try to dress up just a tad higher than what people in the company wear. Don't worry about appearing overdressed for the occasion if you look fresh, polished, and properly dressed. The important thing is to create a lasting impression on the interviewer.

- Make sure you look neat. Never show up in ill-fitting, or wrinkled clothes. Bring a grooming kit with you and step into the comfort room to comb your hair and even brush your teeth if necessary. Do a last-minute look-over in front of the mirror before proceeding to the interview room.

- Choose clothes that make you feel confident and comfortable.

- Avoid revealing types of clothing.

- Select your clothes according to the season and the climate.

- Get your outfit ready the night before the interview.

- You should not wear a cocktail dress, tuxedo, or sequins.

- You should tuck in your shirt. Your shirt should be clean, starched, and unwrinkled.

- You must avoid clothes that are tight or have gaping buttons.

- The pant's waist should sit on your natural waist.

- Do not wear shorts.

- Do not smoke on the day of your meeting with the employers.

- Be sure to brush your teeth properly. Make sure your breath is fresh.

- Do not eat candy or chew gum when you go for an interview.

- For women, try to keep it neat and fixed because you do not want your hair to be covering your eyes while answering your interviewer. For men, get your hair trimmed and have a clean haircut. Groom, if not, shave your facial hair to get that neat appearance on your big day.

- Clean and trim those nails because you do not want unpleasant nails to keep you from nailing that job interview. For the ladies, try to keep it simple with your nail polish and match it with your outfit because you do not want your interview to get distracted by the color of your nails.

- You may or may not wish to wear makeup, however if you do it may be best to opt for the natural look. Again it depends on the position you are applying for and you may wish to use discretion in this regard. The point is not to put all the emphasis how you look as you are there to sell yourself and your attributes.

- Your scent also says something about you and you may try to use it sparingly so that your scent won't linger in the area after you leave.

- Depending on the job and environment you would be working in it may be a good idea to remove your piercings in order to achieve that professional look and in the case of those with tattoos, try to wear something that can cover them up. Of course if you are applying for a job at a tattoo parlor then the above would not apply.

- Try to stay away from loud colors and be as conservative as possible especially for those applying for managerial positions. It is also important to wear something comfortable but not too shabby because when you look good, you will feel good! Check if there are missing buttons and cut those threads hanging from your clothes.

- Do not wear something that's stained and crumpled because it reflects how well you take care of yourself. And do not forget to remove those tags if you bought new clothes for your interview. For men, match your belt with your shoes. The key here is to keep it simple and neat but classy. If you buy a new shirt, be prepared to iron it first rather than wearing it straight from the packet.

- Avoid excessiveness. The best tip for your general appearance during interviews is to avoid anything excessive, men shouldn't drench themselves in cologne, and women, on the other hand, shouldn't overdo their makeup and go overboard with the appearance. It's an interview, not a wedding, so you want to keep it subtle and professional.

- You don't need to buy expensive outfits and jewelry for interviews, because it's not a flaunting contest. Yes, you need to look good, but general cleanliness and neatly pressed clothes will do the trick. You don't want your appearance to take away more than it should from your interview, and the focus should be on what you have to say and your personality rather than your expensive Rolex. So, this another one of those cases where less is more.

- Keep your looks simple and not loud. You wouldn't want your interviewer to be distracted by anything other than your positive personality. Avoid using excessive jewelry, putting on thick makeup, neon-colored hair and fancy, skimpy clothing that shows too much skin. Bring a long a briefcase (or a handbag for the ladies). It will make you look neat and organized.

- Avoid using perfume especially those that have powerful scents. It won't help your cause instead, it will only distract the interviewer who may even be sickened by its puissant scent. In the first place, you would want to be remembered for your skill sets and experience and not for the stench of your perfume.

- Do a dress rehearsal a day before the interview to make sure everything its perfectly. This will give you time to make some changes or adjustments where ever they may be needed.

Chapter 5: Techniques to Make a Winning Interview

As you might expect, the actual interview is a critical part of this entire process. Let's take a look at some topics to consider at this pivotal moment.

Be confident in yourself. If you have landed an interview, the company has already seen promise in you. Now you just have to build upon that and show them what personal advantages you can bring to their business.

First impressions leave a lasting impression so be sure to represent yourself well. Looking them in the eyes and giving a firm handshake is an undervalued way to set yourself apart from the competition.

Smile. A company wants to know that you are going to be a nice, as well as a capable, coworker. Simply smiling can ease any tension in the interview and guide it to a more positive atmosphere.

There are things you should pay close attention to that can make a huge different in your impression on the interviewer.

Confidence

You must come into an interview with confidence. No one wants to hear whining or see someone that clearly does not believe they can do the job. This is a delicate balance because you do not want to be too cocky. You want to be sure of yourself, but not flamboyant about it. The interviewer should know that you are capable of doing the job but will also get along well with your co-workers.

Accomplishments should be factual. You want to list them as a matter-of-fact without a great amount of detail. The interviewer needs to know what they are, but you do not need to brag.

To show your assertiveness, you have to practice being confident. Often, confidence starts with the mindset that you can accomplish all things on your agenda. Being more assertive starts with being proactive about your own life. When you think about what you want to do, then you can set a goal and do it faithfully. That means practicing what you preach. You have to try to do your best at what you do, because then you can be confident. It all starts with being excellent at what you do. However, even then, you can develop confidence when your skill is not the best.

Begin By Getting Good at What You Do

One thing that you have to do is be good at what you do. That will be the first step to a successful interview process. You can not succeed in securing a good job if you're not good at what you do. Even if you do succeed at the interview, you won't last long, if you're not skilled at the job that you want to do. Therefore, it is crucial that you find ways of developing your talent and tailoring your skills to your job. Then, you can have the qualifications necessary to get the job that you want.

Get Qualified and Get the Education You Need

The next step is getting qualified. Go and get that certificate. Get the credentials that you need to confidently submit your resume to the place where you want to work. You will need these things, because when you talk about your experience, then you can bring them up at the interview. Get as many qualifications as you can, because these will enable you to get the interview, and you'll be able to support your candidacy. The more qualified you are, the more confident you will be.

Emphasize Your Strong Points but Don't Gloss Over Your Weaknesses

Now that you are qualified, you should try to emphasize the strong points in your life that you have. Write down all your strengths on a piece of paper, and expand on each of them. Consider them deeply and think about what makes you great at what you do. Then, you can talk about your weaknesses. For every weak point that you have, try to come up with ways that you are handling these weaknesses. Think of ways you're improving yourself or finding ways to get more training and support to help you along the way. It will show some humility and the fact that you want to continually advance in your life.

Do Some Breathing Exercises

Another thing that you should do is some deep breathing. Try to take in as much oxygen as possible before and during the interview. It is important that you are breathing a lot, because that will help you feel better. Also, if you can focus on one thing, it should be breathing in a healthy way. Try doing this, and you should notice how your nerves simply melt away.

Be Positive

Believe that you deserve and are meant to be at the place where you're going to. You should show confidence, and by being positive and having a good mindset, then you'll be ready to show that you know your stuff in the interview. The important thing is to keep your chin up and keep going, even when your body is fighting and making it difficult to function while you're in the interview.

Attitude

Positive attitudes are more alluring than negative ones. You want to smile and be a happy individual to talk to. Avoid frowning and looks of disdain if you hear something that is not what you expected or wanted. Wait for the appropriate time to discuss concerns. This is where behavior comes into play. You do not just have to have the right mental mindset, but display it as well. You may not have a poor attitude but your body language suggests you do. You do not want to send the wrong message by slouching, avoiding eye contact, folding your arms, fiddling with your hair or other objects, speaking inaudibly, or using works such as "like" or "um."

Practicing your interview can help with this and making sure you constantly check your posture can help make sure you give the right message with your body.

Your Body Language

Remember that many employers not only know about body language, but also place as much importance on this as they do the content of your answers. The main indicators of someone being nervous or trying to disguise something are: suddenly changing your seating position (for example, when the interviewer asks an uncomfortable question), constantly touching your face, fiddling with your pen or other objects and shaking your leg.

So that you don't get distracted thinking about how you sit or what gestures you are making when talking, you should practice at home. Sit at a table and ensure that your back and neck are straight, shoulders are relaxed, lower arms are resting on the table and that you are sitting comfortably. Do not interlock your fingers as this can be seen as a sign that you are trying to hide something. Sit like this for a while and memorize this pose. Imagine that you are talking to the interviewer.

Eye Contact

You want to maintain eye contact with the person you are talking to otherwise you appear insecure or rude. You do not want to come off as uninterested as this is the person deciding if you will get the job. You would not appreciate this type of behavior from someone else so do not do look around the room.

Facial Expressions

Your face says a lot about you. Without treading into the unsafe field of first impressions, your face is your entire profile in an interview. It is the first thing people notice when you walk into the room. Your mind, your intellect, your wit, your sense of humor; all come secondary to the onlookers' minds. It is your face that leads everything else.

Your facial expressions cover more than just your eyes, lips and eyebrows. It is how your face as a whole is presented that matters and not just its individual parts. When you have a smiling face, it is natural that those sitting right across the interview table feel good vibes coming from you. On the other hand, a face with a grimace on it is considered cold and unfriendly.

Body Postures

Body postures are all about how you carry yourself. It is the ultimate platform for your body language to be displayed in full vigor.

Sitting is as important as walking. Do not pull the chair out and just assume that you are to sit unless someone asks you to. It is not only against your prospects of landing a job, but also rude to sit down on your own as it gives off an aura of superiority. Wait for one of the interviewers to ask you to sit. Assume a straight posture, with your backbone touching the back of the chair at all points. Do not sit too stiff, as that could lead to cramps and make you nervous eventually.

Do not sit slouching. Straighten up your shoulders a bit and appear smart while doing so. Do not cross your legs under the table. Though most interviewers cannot see what is going on under the table, that position does affect your upper body. One can easily tell how casually your legs are placed under the table by taking a single glance at your upper body.

Do not place one leg above the other while sitting. It shows that you are not just confident about yourself, but also show a general attitude of carelessness towards the interviewers. Behave in a manner that sends the message that you respect them.

Sitting upright in an interview might go in favor of you since it displays an attentive mentality. On the other hand, adopting a slouching position signifies that you are in the mood to hear them out and are only there only to doodle and pass time.

Gestures

In an interview, if you are sitting in a cross-armed position, it implies that you are not welcome to others' point of views and ideas. It displays a cold attitude and often does not come off as desirable. It is a sign of careless confidence to casually fling your arms around while walking. On the other hand, if you clench your fists and walk, it may imply that you are calculated and reserved about yourself.

Hands can be used to convey emotions too. Joining your hands in a Namaste sign shows that you mean respect towards the person. Bowing down is another form of respect followed by the Japanese. If you show someone the 'thumbs up' sign, it means that you are either wishing them good luck or are conveying 'okay' or one of its variants. However, if you do the same in other countries like Iran or Thailand; it can be taken as an equivalent of showing the middle finger in the West.

So, make sure you do not consciously or subconsciously offend your interviewers with your body language or gestures.

Use Appropriate Hand Gestures for Emphasis

Hand gestures improve your communication skills by helping others recognize the impact you wish to make. Hand gestures also enable you to brush off your anxieties and make you more confident because these will let you use your excess energy, which you get whenever you become quite nervous.

Use a Well-Modulated Voice and Practice Vocal Variety

Nobody wants to listen to someone who is monotonous or overly excited. Listen to your voice as you practice your interview answers. Do you sound professional? Is your tone appropriate to the content of your message? When expressing achievement or accomplishment, feel free to use a higher pitch voice that communicates excitement and enthusiasm; meanwhile, when talking about regrets or things that you may have been done better, you can speak more slowly and use a lower-pitched voice.

Respect the Interviewer's Personal Space

Some people like to lean forward while talking and they get lost in their own world while passionately explaining something. Now, while that's okay at times, you need to be careful not to intrude on the interviewer's personal space. If you want to lean forward, do it, but don't get all up in their face! Also, where patting your friend's legs or arms while having a discussion is acceptable, you can never do that in an interview! Remember, this is a professional setting, so act accordingly and keep your reactions under control.

Make Proper Use of Your Hands

I'm not sure what to do with my hands! A problem that faces a lot of people during an interview, although the answer is quite simple. Use them for gestures! Talking while your hands are next to you or motionless makes you look like a robot. So, use your hand gestures while talking. Be careful not to overdo it though; you're not a conductor at the symphony after all. Speaking of hands, never sit with your arms crossed. It implies you're being defensive and non-receptive to what you're being told, even if that is not the case. So, if you often find yourself doing this without noticing, try to keep it in mind during the interview. Also, always keep your palms open. Open palms inspire honesty and authenticity. When you clench them, it implies you have something to hide, or you're dishonest about something.

Nod

It's important that you acknowledge your interviewer when they are speaking to you. A nod every now and then, especially when they say something you agree with, is a sign that you're paying attention. But you should be careful not to do it all the time, regardless of what is being said and how you feel about it. If you do that, you come off looking like a fool with no personality whatsoever. So, never nod aimlessly throughout the interview, and do it only when they're saying something you actually agree with.

Avoid Any Nervous Reflex

You have to be extremely self-aware during the interview to avoid any nervous reflex actions that you might usually show. Don't tap the table with your nails or grab one of those pens and start clicking it. Things like this can be extremely distracting to everyone in the room, not to mention just plain annoying! Compose yourself in a calm manner and avoid tense movements with your hands or legs in general. You should also avoid touching yourself a lot throughout the interview. To elaborate a bit more on this bizarre sentence, some people play with their hair when talking or touch their nose or ears like a soothing mechanism. You should do your best to avoid those ticks as much as possible because they give off the impression that you're insecure or too nervous.

Be Careful When Crossing Your Legs

Some people take offense when sitting across someone cross-legged, and others don't care. This is why it's best to play it safe and avoid doing it. But what do you do if the interview takes time and your legs start feeling numb? Be honest. Ask the interviewer's permission for a second to get up and stretch. They'll appreciate your honesty and might even mirror what you do.

Watch Your Tone

Your tone is very important, and it's considered a part of your body language. You could be saying some very interesting stuff, but saying it in monotonously will take much of its intrigue and probably make the interviewer drowsy. Vary your tone and know when to go higher or lower according to the emotion you're trying to convey. It makes a lot of difference in how your speech is perceived overall.

Learn to be comfortable with silence.

There are times in the interview when your interviewer may seem to fall silent as he reads over your resume, reflects on your answers or writes something down. When this happens, don't feel pressured to fill in the silence. You don't have to keep the conversation going; show confidence in silence.

Maintain Good Eye Contact

Look your interviewer in the eye, as you shake their hand and maintain regular eye contact with them through the interview. However, do not make it overly persistent to appear like you are staring or intimidating. Constant eye contact is considered to be an attempt of intimidation and can make your interviewer uncomfortable. It's okay to look away whenever you feel like you have been staring intently for long.

Lean in Slightly from Time to Time

Leaning forward in your chair as you converse with someone shows that you are interested and engaged in the discussion; therefore, you can lean in towards your interviewer from time to time to portray interest.

However, be careful not to lean too far over the table, as this could crowd the interviewer's personal space and seem intrusive. Note that personal space extends to about 20 inches. Encroaching on this space is an invasion on their space and you will make them feel uncomfortable, which is likely to distract them from your conversation – if you had started to make a really good point, it will be lost.

Smile

A smile is a positive gesture that can immediately create a positive environment. You want an environment with positive vibes, so give a genuine smile. Further, a smile is contagious and soon everyone in the room will catch the positivity. However, do not overdo it otherwise you will seem corny. However, don't overdo it by laughing or grinning throughout the whole thing. Exercise good judgment and smile when you deem it appropriate or when the interviewer is smiling. Try to find the right balance between smiling and being serious, depending on the situation.

Address Everyone

In cases where there is more than one interviewer, be sure to address all of them with your gaze moving from time to time before you bring back your attention to the person who asked you a question. Keep in mind that you will need all of their votes (yes, even from the mean looking one) to get the job.

Be Sure to Listen

In the same way that you should be confident in using silence, be a good listener, too. Instead of consistently worrying about what you're supposed to say, pay attention to what the other person is saying so that you can respond properly. Keep in mind that you want your interviewer to see you as a professional who he may likely want to work with, so your likeability matters, too. By nodding your head, keeping eye contact and listening to what he says, he gets the impression that you respect his ideas and that while you are confident, you are definitely not arrogant. In addition, try not to interrupt your interviewer for the duration of your interview. This is a skill you need to learn as well.

Express Gratitude

Gratitude may also exhibit confidence. Thank your interviewer for taking the time to review your application and meet up with you. An interviewer appreciates a candidate who appreciates his efforts as well. Remember, your feelings and attitudes towards another person will likely be similar to the other person's feelings and attitudes towards you. So even if you don't really like your interviewer that much, treat him as you would an important client or customer, striving to make him feel good about himself. You are likely to win him over when you do this.

Non-verbal communication is a huge component of your overall communication impact. Nothing can be more powerful than a communicator whose message content is consistent with delivery. So from now on, practice becoming a better communicator. You can practice in front of a mirror, or in front of a friend. You can also record your voice and listen to it. You can even videotape yourself to get a better observation of how you can further improve at communicating confidence.

Principles of Interview Etiquette

Your etiquette determines whether or not you get to the next level of the recruitment process. Most job candidates spend much of their time and energy thinking about their skills and qualifications to present to the interviewer and forget about personal conduct. Good manners determine the success of a business relationship since they determine how you establish rapport with other people.

The following guidelines reflect the principles of interview etiquette that show you how to avoid some mistakes job hunters have made and which derail them from reaching their goal.

How to Greet Your Interviewers?

Interviewers are most often referred to by their first name. Chances of offending someone by referring to them by their first name are minimal since it is the universal standard of meeting someone for the first time. However, calling someone by their last name shows a sense of respect and it directly tells them that you consider them important. Remember that the employer is looking for suggestions that you will be easy to work with, fully understanding the organizational management structure and respecting it.

Table Talk

After greeting, the interviewer should remain standing until or unless you are asked to sit. Once you are offered a seat, refrain from feeling comfortable to the point of placing your belongings, such as a handbag, on the table. Be humble enough to place them under your chair or beside your legs. Only a professional binder should be placed on the table near you. Remember to turn down the offer of a drink politely if one is offered. Finally, sit up properly without moving your feet around.

Ensure Your Cell Phone is Completely Off

An interview is definitely one of the most crucial gatherings in your life and a phone distraction is not worth ruining such a meeting. Interviewers are keen to notice a phone's vibration; thus, it should be totally off. If possible, do not enter the interview room with your phone. At this moment there is nothing more important than your conversation with your potential employer. They will want to know if you can serve their clients without being distracted by your own personal gadget. Therefore, make sure to avoid the distraction at all costs.

Do Not Talk Over the Speaker

The most disturbing aspect in an interview is stepping into the interviewer's last two to three words of a statement and talking over without even extending the courtesy to letting them finish their statement.

Act Like You Care

Some interviewees mistakenly believe that the 'I don't give a damn' attitude inspires confidence and boosts your chances of getting the job. It doesn't, and it won't. When you act like you don't really care about the job and the company, you come off as repulsive and annoying; definitely not confident. So, always behave like you really want the job, and that you're willing to do everything it takes to get it, even if that is not necessarily the case. If you manage to sell that, your chances of being hired to become exponentially better.

Chase the Position Tirelessly Even If You Feel Like the Interview Has Already Gone Wrong

It is not unusual for someone to be having a rough time during an interview and to even create conclusions about the company, which may impact their ability to deliver the best version of themselves. The best thing you can do during such a time is to maintain professionalism and finish the interview without showing any signs of backing down. Remember you are not being forced to take this job, after all. You are still in the driver's seat in the end since you can always turn down an offer or respectfully withdraw from the process. Job candidates can be fond of prejudice toward the interviewers and they end up regretting it later. Ensure that you have collected all possible facts before making an ultimate judgment about the organization. Leave the interviewers with a good impression of you as it could pay back later in unimaginable ways. Imagine having poorly interviewed with this employer's biggest client who is now your boss.

Maintain Positive Language

To maintain a positive language, the first thing you should never do is badmouth anyone. Not your former bosses, colleagues, company, family, or the guy who sells hotdogs on the corner. Why? Because there are two sides to any story, and when you talk ill of someone, a smart interviewer will want to know the other side of the story. They'll assume that the problem might be you. If you mention former colleagues, managers, and companies in a poor manner, any sane person would be wise enough to check out your story. Are you really trying to convince them that your luck was so bad, you only worked with awful people? This is why badmouthing others gives a very bad impression, and it seriously jeopardizes your chances of ever getting the job.

Use the Interviewer's Name

You form a sort of bond for the duration of the interview as you call each other by your names. There are even studies that claim you seem more confident and composed when you use somebody's name while talking to them. What do you do if you're terrible at remembering names? Well, when you first hear their names, make sure you got it right. If you didn't quite catch it, be sure to ask them about it again until you're certain – it definitely beats staying quiet and then mispronouncing their name during the interview. Then, you need to keep telling it to yourself for a few minutes until you get the hang of it, and more importantly, use it while talking to them in the first ten minutes. It'll stick that way, and you will never forget it during the remainder of the interview.

Remember that Your Interview is Not Over Until You Walk Out of the Gate

From the moment you walk through the gate, how you talk to the receptionist or any other person, including the premises' cleaners, matters a lot in your hiring process. Some employers have taken time to ask parties such as the receptionist how you greeted them on your way in. Hiring managers could watch a candidate as they exit the interview premises. Conversely, some interviewees have some outrageous behavior such as starting to make calls or lighting up cigarettes right outside the premises. Remember to maintain official conduct until you are far from the premises.

Close the Interview the Right Way

Express your gratitude toward the interviewer for the interview as it comes to an end and restate your interest in the role. Feel free to make an inquiry on how long it would take before they could reach out. Finally, greet everyone in the room by the hand if possible and also use their name as this shows your attention to details and courtesy. Greeting other people in the outer office shows good manners as well, although it may not be a strategy per se. Remember to keep smiling until you leave the premises.

Send a Thank You Note After the Interview

Thanking the hiring manager for the interview counts as an important part of your etiquette principles. It reminds the interviewers about you and shows them how courteous you are. Also, take this chance to clarify anything you feel you need to reiterate. Refer to anything that the interviewer said during the interview that intrigued you. Reiterate why you think you are fit for the position.

Control Your Anxiety

It is normal to feel nervous during an interview especially if you are badly in need of the job; however, you have to manage your anxiety during an interview because nervousness often accompanies anxiety.

This can show in the interview through gestures such as trembling legs, excessive sweating, etc.

An excellent way to alleviate anxiety is to make it your friend. Moreover, speak clearly and at a moderate pace when you are in the interview room. This ensures the interviewers understand you well and helps project confidence. You can also gargle lukewarm water before going for an interview. This helps clear your throat, so your voice stays crisp and clear during the interview.

When you take care of yourself well, you will feel more comfortable and everything else follows. When you're comfortable, your interviewer will also feel comfortable talking to you.

It is normal for a person to feel stress when attending an interview. What is not normal is not feeling it at all like you don't care that you have a job interview to pass or you are convinced you will get the job. Stress during job interviews is inevitable. For many people, it can be the most nerve-wracking thing to experience in their entire life and especially those attending their first ever job interview. It is therefore important that you know how to handle stress and here are some ways to beat it:

You know that you have to prepare and practice for that big day but don't take it too seriously that you forget to give yourself time to rest. Go out for a walk. Jog if you must. Watch your favorite series. Hang out with your friends. The key here is that you have to find a way to distract yourself a little and enjoy life a little bit more. Treat yourself to a massage.

When you're anxious and stressed, you tend to breathe faster and shallower. Calm yourself by breathing more deeply and a little bit slower. Concentrate on your breathing. It will take the focus away from your stress.

Chapter 6: Winning Interview by Phone or Skype

This interview is quite tricky, because you want to be relaxed and feel that you are doing a good job at it, but you don't want to be too casual. If you are interviewing for a company, it is important to put on your best dress, because that will show that you are a serious candidate. If you are doing the interview in your home, try to not have many distractions in the background. The best backdrop for your interview would be a plain white background, but sometimes this is not possible. However, as long as your apartment or home is clean and tidy, it should not be a problem if you have another type of background in view.

In addition to the background and location where you will have your Skype interview, you need to make sure your camera is working properly and that the sound is functioning well. This is crucial, because you don't want to have technical difficulties occur during the interview, although this can inevitably happen, even when you're over-prepared. You should try to prepare for this well in advance so you can be ready to start at the right time.

Put your notes within your reach; however, refrain from putting them in a place that will be visible to the eyes of the interviewer. You don't want to make it look like you are reading a script; that will be an automatic turn-off to the interviewer. You want to make sure you are talking naturally. So, have a few notes available in case you blank, but don't stare at a piece of paper while you're doing it.

For a Skype interview, it is crucial that you look into the camera, because that will show sincerity and eye contact with the screen which may be crucial to scoring you more points. The better your on-camera appearance, the more likely you are to move on to the next round of interviews if it includes an in-person component.

When the call is being made, you should know if the employer will call you and prepare for it. Know ahead of time who is going to initiate the call and be ready for the moment to answer the call immediately.

Once you have entered the call, the interview process begins. You have to be on your best behavior throughout the call. Try not to fidget or make too many exaggerated body language cues, and don't smile too much. It is important to look relaxed and confident but not to swagger or use your hands a lot during a Skype interview. Instead, you should be calm and avoid doing too much on the screen. There are limits to the Skype screen, and you have to use it to your advantage rather than to your detriment. There is only so much that the interviewer can see of you. For one, they can only see your upper body. However, that doesn't mean you need to wear a suit jacket and be in shorts or boxers while you're talking to the interviewer. You need to prepare for this interview as if it were a formal interview. Therefore, you must be completely dressed and ready to do well during the process.

Note the timing of the interview. If it is going on longer than expected, then you will know that you are a top candidate and that the interviewer is looking upon you favorably. The average Skype interview can take between 20 and 40 minutes, though, at times, they can last up to an hour. Typically, if your interview is under time, you will expect that it will not have a good outcome. If an interviewer likes you, then they will want to spend more time reviewing your application and going over your profile. They will show genuine interest in you, because they want to hire you. Take going over the time as a sign that your application is going to get good marks.

You have some research to do before you're ready for that phone interview, so you need to buy yourself some time. Try to schedule the phone interview for the following day.

Now hop on the Internet and learn everything you can about the company that's contacting you. If it's a headhunter calling, they won't likely tell you their client's name, because the headhunter only makes his commission if he successfully places you in that position. And the only way he can do that is by not having you contact the hiring employer directly. You should, however, ask the headhunter for any information s/he can give you on the employer so you can be prepared for the interview. You should be able to get at least the type of business it is, how large (revenue and/or employees), general location, etc.

Assuming you have the name of the company for whom you'd actually be working, find their website and read it – all – especially the About Us page. Studying the website carefully will help you understand the employer from the employer's point of view, which is important. You need to know about their history, their target clients, and their core business. You need to know what they think of themselves and what they say are their strengths.

Now look the company up on Indeed and see what the company's employees are saying about working there. If most of the reviews are negative, I suggest you do the phone interview but let the interviewer know you've researched the company and you're concerned that the company's employees don't have much positive to say about it. If nothing else, it's interesting to see how the employer will spin negative reviews. They may claim it's just "disgruntled ex-employees", but some thoughts to keep in mind.

How do they know these are "disgruntled employees", when the reviews are confidential?

If their ex-employees are disgruntled there are likely valid reasons for that. See if you can pick up any themes that seem consistent across most of the negative reviews. For example, if seven former employees wrote negative reviews about the company and four or five of those reviews mentioned the company's dictatorial management style, there's a good chance the overall management style of the company is rather dictatorial. Where there's smoke, there's usually fire.

If ten former employees took the time to write reviews about the company and seven of them were negative, chances are good that there are three times that number of disgruntled current and former employees who didn't bother to write reviews.

Today, we have a limitless ability to write online reviews about everything from an interview experience to a handyman's handiwork to a new restaurant you tried to the comfort of the new socks you purchased. We're constantly online, giving our opinions on everything – and the subjects of our opinions are mostly either the Greatest Ever or the Worst Ever.

Your goal here is not to challenge the employer on the reviews, and you definitely don't want to alienate your potential employer. But you do need to find out whether you'll be walking headfirst into a hornet's nest if you take a job with them.

Now you've got the information you need to have that phone interview, if you choose to do so. If you've learned a lot more negative than positive about the employer, you may want to reconsider. You're not going to be able to overcome the inertia of an unhappy employee population or change a company's overall culture, so why even subject yourself to it? If you feel uneasy about what you've learned about the employer, the best advice is to avoid them. Call the recruiter back, thank them for the opportunity to interview for the position, but say you don't believe it would be a good fit for you and you want to be respectful of the interviewer's time.

Make Your Surroundings Ideal

Even though you can conduct a phone interview right in the comfort of your home, it is still wise to make your surroundings as suitable as possible. Doing this will relax your body and clear your mind so that you can answer even the toughest questions from your interviewer.

Dress for Success

First, dress as if you are going to a real interview. Now, you might find this tip unusual since you'll only be at home, but it can help boost your confidence. Dressing up lets you simulate the situation—making you more likely to act and respond like you are in the hiring manager's office. Also, be sure to sit upright during the call so you can concentrate better and exude confidence.

Choose a Quiet Room

Set the call up in a room where there are entirely no distractions. It should be just you and the things you need, like your desk, pen, résumé, notepad, list of interview questions, bottle of water (in case your throat gets dry), and so forth. The room should also be well-ventilated to help you relax during the conversation.

Get Computer Access If Possible

Have your computer and Internet connection ready as well. You'll never know when you might need look to up information that can assist you with the interview.

Use a Landline for the Interview

If possible, use a landline to achieve a more stable reception. Cellphones are often prone to connection problems, and a disrupted call can irritate employers. Surely, you do not want that to happen! It is safer to talk via landline, but if you do not have one, see to it that you are in a room with a good reception for your mobile phone.

Sell Yourself

Now that you are done learning the first three parts of a successful interview, you can finally proceed to step four, selling yourself effectively. This part is often tricky because when you are trying to promote yourself, you can easily sound like you are bragging. The key is balance: market your personality, skills and experiences, but do not overdo it. Turning off your potential employer is the last thing you want to do, especially in this very crucial stage of the hiring process. This fourth chapter will teach you how to promote yourself the right way so can stand out from the rest of the job applicants.

Stay Positive

Suitable candidates always stay positive. They know how stressful and nerve-wracking an interview can be, yet they are wise enough not to let it get the best of them. Being positive is essential from the very beginning—even when you are still preparing for an interview.

Having an optimistic outlook in life motivates you to do your best, and it makes all your efforts worthwhile, so that even if you do not get the job, you will not be upset because you've learned from the experience. When you are positive, you are also able to relax more during the interview and achieve better results. So work on adapting an optimistic mindset, not just for the interview, but for your entire life as well. Soon enough, you'll attract plenty of wonderful opportunities for yourself!

Make a Good First Impression

This phrase may be cliché, but there's a reason it is always repeated: it works. So many applicants take this for granted—they do not seem to understand the impact of an employer's phone call, so they do not even make an effort to behave professionally. When this happens, it can be downhill from there.

Now, if you are really interested in landing that position, you should work on creating a lasting impression. There are three primary areas you should focus on:

- **Politeness.** Observe proper phone etiquette. For instance instead of saying, "Hello," when the phone rings, answer as if you are already working in the office. Say, "Hi, this is (state your name)" and you'll be on a good start. For the rest of the call, be polite by addressing your interviewer by their title (Mr., Ms., Prof., Dr.,) and surname, until they tell you otherwise.

- **Tone of Voice**. As the interview is conducted through the phone, the tone of your voice will play a significant role in your success. Your tone of voice is one of the first things that your prospective employer will notice, so always sound sincere and interested, rather than slow and distracted. Pay attention to the clarity of your words as well, to avoid being asked to repeat yourself.

- **Personality**. Don't forget to let your personality shine! Most applicants tend to sound robotic when they converse on the phone, and that makes for a very boring interview. Keep in mind that hiring managers are people too, so there's no need to be anxious. It is okay to show who you are, because that is what employers want to get a sense of during the call.

So as soon as you pick up the phone, apply these three basic tips and make a good first impression. When you succeed in responding correctly, speaking clearly and cheerfully, and being likeable, you will improve the likelihood of getting a callback from your potential employer.

Emphasize Your Skills

At some point during the interview, you will be asked what skills you can contribute to the company. This is your chance to emphasize your work experiences, special skills, achievements, and work performance, but try not to do this in a way that makes you seem arrogant. Simply state what makes you the best choice among the other candidates and sell yourself without bragging too much.

Know How to Answer Common Interview Questions

As mentioned in the first chapter, it is important that you familiarize yourself with the basic interview questions. Many candidates get rattled when asked simple questions like "Tell me about yourself" and "Where do you see yourself in five years?" However, if you have done your homework and prepared great answers, you'll certainly gain an edge and impress the hiring manager.

Be Prepared to Explain

Part of the interview may also involve explaining your past work experiences. Anticipate being asked about gaps in employment history, being fired by an employer (if applicable), reasons for leaving your previous position. An employer may also ask if you have ever been in a particular situation, and how you responded to it. Recall your experiences well and be prepared to give good examples.

Know Your Strengths and Weaknesses

Last, be aware of your strengths and weaknesses. While you want to highlight your abilities, you should also recognize the areas that you need to improve on—but do it in a way that won't cost you the job. For instance, instead of saying that you are bad at presentations, you could say that sometimes you get nervous talking in front of people. Don't be one of those applicants who say that their problem is they "work too hard" when asked about their weaknesses. Admitting some of your shortcomings will make you seem genuine, but assure your interviewer though that you are willing to improve yourself.

Things You Should Never Do During a Phone Interview

So you are in the middle of an interview for the job you really want, and everything is going smoothly. You prepared for the call, answered all the questions and even charmed the interviewer. Then suddenly, you say something and everything goes wrong. What happened? How did a seemingly successful interview go down the drain just like that? For many applicants, a simple word or gesture can change the course of an entire conversation. One minute they are on a roll, and the next they wished the call would just end.

Terrible interviews happen all the time, but there are many ways to keep you from experiencing them. It is important to understand that just as there are basic rules to follow during a phone interview, there are also specific guidelines to observe on what **not** to do. In this chapter, you'll learn all the things you should not do or say during the call. Carefully read the following lists of interview no-no's in this chapter so you can consciously prevent them from ruining your chances of getting a job.

- Don't be tardy for the scheduled call – that will automatically give the interviewer a wrong impression of you.

- Don't be unprepared – as mentioned in the previous chapters, preparation is not just essential but rather necessary for a good interview.

- Don't answer "hello" when picking up the phone for an interview – always introduce yourself properly and politely.

- Don't overthink the questions – it will only make you lose your concentration and set off your nerves.

- Don't lie and make up stories just to impress the interviewer – believe me, they will see through you.

- Don't brag – know the difference between projecting positive confidence and being arrogant.

- Don't say you know how to do something when you don't – you'll only be misleading the employer, and they'll expect more from you if you do get the job.

- Don't tell jokes (especially inappropriate ones) and use dry wit in your humor – jokes can easily be misunderstood and make you sound sarcastic even if you do not mean to.

- Don't smoke, drink alcohol, chew gum or eat candy at any time during the interview – be professional even if it is only a phone call.

- Don't act bored or tired – this will make your prospective employer think that you do not really want the job.

- Don't discuss politics, religion, race, sexuality and other sensitive topics – it can create tension between you and the interviewer.

- Don't make negative comments about your previous job, company, boss and colleagues – just say it did not work out for you and you are looking for a new place where you can realize your full potential.

- Don't get too comfortable with the interviewer – remember, he or she will determine whether you are fit for the job. Getting too casual and informal will make you seem immature and unprepared.

- Don't refer to yourself in the third person – it may confuse your interview.

- Don't ask about work benefits, salary, and other financial concerns yet – telephone interviews are primarily meant to sort out undesirable applicants. You can inquire about salaries and benefits later.

- Don't respond to questions with a simple **yes** and **no** – always expand your answers and give examples if necessary.

- Don't shout at your kids or pets while on the phone – this means you are not really focusing on the call. Stay in a room without any kinds of distractions.

- Don't answer the doorbell – your guests can wait, but this interview will only happen once if you do not do well.

- Don't be rude if things don't go your way – just be cool and keep your composure no matter what.

- Don't ask how well you did on the interview – when the call ends, just be polite and thank the hiring manager for calling you. Asking about your performance will make you seem desperate.

Know When to Draw the Line

While there are many things you should do on a phone interview, there are also several things you should never do. Knowing the difference will help you achieve a flawless conversation with your potential boss, so make sure to learn all these telephone interview no-noes' for your own good. They can help you succeed and keep the phone call from turning into a major disaster.

Chapter 7: What to Do in a Winning Interview

Practice Speaking Clearly

Some people tend to mumble when they get nervous and aside from handling stress properly, it is just as important to practice speaking. Here are some tips to a clearer conversation with your interviewer.

Take a Deep Breath and Prepare for Battle

Before you arrive at the interview venue, you should prepare your breathing, because that will be a key part of your well-being once you get there. You need to be breathing well and should take in some deep breaths to take in as much oxygen as possible. The worst thing that could happen is that you could pass out at the interview and have to go to the emergency room. You definitely don't want that to happen. Try your best to take those deep breaths and keep it going for a while.

Go to the Bathroom at Least a Few Times Beforehand

If you need to go to the bathroom, you should try to go at least a few times before you get into your interview. Don't drink too much coffee or too many liquids prior to arriving at the interview. It will only aggravate your digestive system and make you want to go to the bathroom frequently. Try to go to visit the restroom and get everything out before you go into the interview.

Freshen Up in the Bathroom

After going to the bathroom, you should freshen up by putting on cologne, combing your hair, and brushing your teeth. If you are a woman, you might want to touch up your make-up if you are wearing it. Do whatever it takes to prepare well to go into the interview. It will also make you feel better when you go in.

Give Yourself a Pep Talk

This point is big. Only you can encourage yourself and give yourself the most pep talk to get you going through the interview. So, you're going to have to exclaim self-affirmation and compliments to get yourself prepped and ready to go into with a battle mentality and an "I can do it" attitude that is going to blow away everyone in the room. You have to tell yourself how great you are and show it, because you want your presence to command the whole room and impress the interviewer. Say things like the following:

Giving yourself pep talk helps to calm the nerves, because then you can focus on pumping yourself up. Although the adrenaline is flowing like crazy, you will feel that you can manage your stress and get going as fast as possible. Your nerves may be a bit high, but then, you can tackle the problem head on and do some mental exercises that will strengthen your brain and help you overcome any anxiety you are feeling.

Drink a Bottle or Two of Water to Maintain Hydration

In addition to these tips, you should drink some water before your interview. There's nothing worse than arriving at the interview and feeling thirsty, so you should try to drink as much as possible without having to go to the bathroom. Try to be hydrated before entering the room. In some cases, interviewers will give a glass of water to the candidate, but you should definitely not count on it and get your own water to keep yourself hydrated.

Look at Your Notes, But Don't Cram

You may have prepared notes or other points to think about as you were preparing for the interview, but you should not cram any information in your head before, as this is counterproductive. Instead, prepare what you will say when you meet the interviewer, and practice delivering your first speech or introduction that you will say to him or her. It's important to have this information readily available so you don't stumble through what you're going to say. Be sure to memorize some of your dialogue.

Warm Up Your Voice so You Don't Have a Frog in Your Throat

Another thing you can do is warm up your voice, especially in the morning. You don't want to have a frog in your throat prior to going into the interview. Try to prepare well for this part. You can gargle with some water or something else to provide hydration for your throat. This way, you can freely express yourself at the interview.

Maintain Good Posture

Aside from making you look confident, maintaining a good posture will help you in terms of breathing resulting in better speech. Sit up straight and tuck your stomach in. Just be careful to not look like you are posing for a modeling competition.

Be Aware of How Fast You Talk

A lot of people speak fast whenever they're nervous and practicing slower speech results in a much clearer and more comprehensible speech during an interview.

Listen

Listen to how people talk on the television or radio. Try to observe how they pronounce their words and how fast they talk.

Be Nice to the Receptionist and Waiters

Interview aside, you should always be nice to people, regardless of what their job may be. At a company location, chances are you will be greeted by a receptionist, and then a waiter will come to ask you if you would like a drink. Needless to say, you should be nice to them because it's the right thing to do, and because if some of the interviewers spot you being rude or disrespectful, you will be blacklisted before they even meet you in person. Nobody likes to work with someone who's rude or impolite. You'd be surprised how far manners can get you in this world.

Smile and Shake the Interviewer's Hands

The power of a smile is magical, and it shows in interviews. If you walk into one frowning and wearing a long face, you will probably make the interviewers uneasy and uncomfortable. Besides, a smile is just contagious, and you have no idea how much positivity and glee you could be spreading! So, make sure you spread that kind of energy walking into an interview. You should also shake hands, firmly, unless you know of some religious exceptions that might not warrant you doing so – in some religions, women don't prefer to shake hands with men and vice versa. In a special case as that,

94

wait for them to extend their hand rather than taking the initiative yourself. If that is not the case, then offer your hand first and get off to a good start. A smile and a strong handshake give a positive vibe and a great first impression that you will want in your interview.

Don't Focus Your Attention on Just One Person

It's possible that you will be interviewed by more than one person. In cases like these, you can't just pay attention to one of the people sitting in the room, even if they were asking most of the questions. You need to divide your attention across everybody in the room because the person asking the questions might not even have a say in the hiring decision.

Don't Be Too Friendly!

Yes, it's important to build a rapport and get to know the interviewer, but you also need to be professional and detached. You want them to like you, but that shouldn't come at the expense of your professional image. Do you need to be humorous? Sure, why not, but as long as it's within boundaries and doesn't go too far. You can make a witty remark here or there, yet telling inappropriate jokes or getting far too comfortable with the interviewer might backfire more times than not.

Relax

You can try all the techniques mentioned earlier to calm yourself before an interview and still find yourself agitated when in the spotlight, and that might cause a lot of problems. Being nervous in the middle of an interview means you will probably fluster while answering questions, and you will come off as a person who's not confident, or worse, trying to hide something.

So, control your emotions once the interview has started and kept your thoughts in check. Focus on listening to each question and answering the best way possible. That way, you will be able to remain calm and go through the interview with little to no issues.

Bring Your Resume With You

While it is customary for interviewers to print out your resume before they meet you, sometimes they forget, or the printer might be malfunctioning. To err on the side of caution, bring it along with you in case they don't have it – opening a resume and scrolling through it on a phone or laptop is pretty annoying. Besides, it shows that you've come prepared for the occasion, and that reflects on your ability to foresee problems and be ready with their solutions. Always a good thing!

Bring Along Any Relevant Material

Got your portfolio printed and prepared in a nice, chic folder? Bring it along. Whatever props you deem relevant or necessary to the interview or the job, bring them along, and you will have thoroughly impressed your interviewer. Doing something like this shows you're proactive and that you're a person who takes the initiative without the need for someone to tell them, and that's a trait interviewers look for and admire.

Open Your Mouth a Little Wider

Those words won't come out as you want them to if you are not opening your mouth enough so practice talking and observe yourself if you've been pronouncing words properly. We are not talking about cheesy wide mouthed enunciation, but do not talk with your lips almost pressed together. You will mumble and not be heard clearly.

Speak a Little Bit Louder

When you speak louder, you are not simply easier to comprehend but also, it makes you have better articulation so speak a little bit slower resulting in a clearer speech. Remember not to be too loud that you sound like you are shouting at your interviewer.

Talk With Confidence

The tone of your voice is just as important as your choice of words. Aside from looking confident, you also have to sound like you really are and here are some tips in order for you to achieve that.

Pause

When asked a question, it is not wrong to pause for a few seconds to gather your thoughts. This will also signal that you are really thinking of what to answer and not just telling them a load of nonsense. Just be careful not to pause too long that it makes your interview process stagnant. You do not want your interviewer to get bored.

Work On Your Tone

Do not raise your voice because you do not want to look angry. Speak in a tone that would make you sound interested. Do not stick to the same tone in all your responses so as not to seem like you just want to get things over with as soon as possible.

Use Absolute Words

Avoid saying "I hope to...", "I believe...", and "I think...". Start you responses with "I am...", "I will..." and "I can..." to prevent sounding uncertain of what you are saying. They want someone who is assertive, confident, and sure of what they are saying.

Be Comfortable

It is important that you feel and look comfortable because it helps for a smooth interview-interviewee relationship. It makes the interviewer ask and discover your good qualities more easily. Remember that you are not at home, therefore do not slouch and look lazy or overly comfortable. Be careful not to lean across the chair. The key here is you have to be open for communication and be able to deliver your responses with ease.

Walking

As soon as that door opens, the interviewer starts observing you and how you walk is also part of their assessment. Show your confidence and that you feel good about yourself by walking straight towards the interviewer with that back straightened and chin up. Try to keep a balance between looking too lousy and overconfident.

Making Hand Gestures

When you're nervous, you tend to have shaky hands and might consider hiding them but that is not the way to go. Shake off that nervousness by making them involved during the interview process. Use hand gestures when you respond to your interviewer. And as much as possible, try to make gestures where the interview can see you palms because it signifies that you are being open.

Making Eye Contact

Maintaining good eye contact shows how sincere and interested you are but do not stare at your interviewer the entire time. Try to look at different parts of the interviewer's face every few seconds.

Sitting Straight

This is a no-brainer but oftentimes taken for granted. When we feel pressure, we tend to forget noticing our posture. Try to rest back on your seat to look like you are comfortable with your interview but also remember not to slouch. Also, do not forget to sit only when you are asked to. Leaning towards the interviewer shows how interested you are in the conversation. Try not to lean too close that it looks unprofessional!

Smiling

Show your interviewer how friendly and pleasant you are by smiling but do not force a smile so practicing beforehand will help. As soon as you step inside the company's premises, smile or greet everyone in order to gain their approval even before your interview starts.

During your interview, they are thinking about whether you are the right fit for the company's culture and for their team. Are you someone they want working for them? They're also thinking about how you will handle meeting tight deadlines and the increased stress of new challenges. You need to present yourself as someone they will be comfortable spending lots of time with at work. Otherwise, you risk not being considered for the next step in the process. Since you often spend more time with the people you work with than with your own family, it is crucial that the interviewer likes you. The interviewer understands there may be times you will be asked to work 10, 12, 14 hour days to meet an important deadline. You must show that you can help create a positive work environment.

Smile throughout the interview when you're answering questions. Also, when you are listening. You want to smile to show your engagement with the interviewer. Be sure that your outward appearance is open and inviting. Smiling is one way that you can achieve that.

Giving a Good Hand Shake

Practice your handshake with a friend or relative in order to achieve that perfect handshake! Remember not to make it too light or too tight.

Observing

When somebody else walks in, nod and make eye contact to the person because this might just be your future co-worker! Show how easy you are to work with by acknowledging their presence.

This is also a way to find out things that you can give compliments about.

Leaving

When the interviewer signals the end try not to leave right away. Give yourself a few seconds before standing up and do not hurry. Take your time but also do not be too slow to leave. Be careful especially in closing the door because you do not want your last move to be banging a door at the end of your interview.

Shake With Power

Another often overlooked component of every interview is your handshake. Don't make the mistake of taking your handshake for granted. Are you absolutely confident your handshake is strong? Seriously, I'm not joking. I'm absolutely serious. Have you ever experienced an awkward handshake? Don't worry. I have an easy to tip you can implement to ensure each and every handshake you give is high quality.

Are you ready? First, grab a partner. As you begin to lean over and extend your right arm, make an effort to extend your thumb straight up in the air. This should be a slightly more exaggerated movement to you; however, no one will ever notice. Then, as your palm makes contact with the other person, let the other person close their grip first.

Be Assertive

To be considered a top candidate, you need to demonstrate a certain level of assertiveness during the interview.

Research shows companies place higher value on employees who are able to take action to get things accomplished. Before your interview ends, you must make sure you have sufficiently addressed all of the interviewers' major concerns.

Strategic Listening

Listening is easy. However, being an active and engaged listener is challenging, especially during an interview. Do not formulate your response to a question while an interviewer is still talking. If you do, you risk losing focus on the interviewer and what he or she is communicating. When you are thinking of the next things you want to say, you are not fully present in the moment. Instead, pay attention to the specific language that the interviewer is using. Are there key words or phrases he or she continues to use? If you are able to use his or her own words in your responses, you will connect with your interviewer on a deeper, subconscious level.

Sounds easy enough, doesn't it? Well, think again. A lot of people fall prey to the whole 'lost in your own thoughts' trap. This could be because you're trying to prepare your answers before the questions are asked, or because you haven't rested or prepared enough before the interview. One of the worst things you could do to an interviewer is to make them feel like what they're saying isn't important and that you're not paying attention. You have to actively listen to each question you're being asked and answer based on that. This is a conversation, not a quiz, and memorizing answers to just spill them out during an interview won't get you anywhere. You have to show them that you're an active listener because this is one of the most important qualities hiring managers look for in an employee.

You should show an authentic interest in the interviewer. This can be achieved by using appropriate body language. In addition to smiling, you should make eye contact between 60–70% of the time and nod your head at key points made by the interviewer. Go even further by sitting up straighter or even on the edge of your chair when he or she makes key points about the role and responsibilities.

Competent Communicator

In your answers, be sure to demonstrate exactly how you can fulfill the requirements of the job. To gain an unfair advantage from your competition, you need to provide detailed examples of your relevant accomplishments. A common interview mistake is for a job seeker to ramble on and on and on and on and eventually go off-topic, never completely addressing the original question. You can easily prevent this from happening to you if you stick to communicating a maximum of three main points for each response.

Be sure to highlight your previous experience and how the skills you have developed can help the company.

Advance Mirroring Techniques

These techniques will help you connect with your interviewers on a deeper level. On a subconscious level. Take a moment and think of your most meaningful relationship: with your best friend, a loving family member, or significant other. Now recall the last interaction you had in person. How was your communication style and your body language? Most likely your body language was open and inviting. You might be surprised that you were copying the exact body position of the other person. Can you remember if you both were holding your arms in the same way or maybe your hand gestures were similar? For sure, I'd bet that your legs and feet were facing each other. During your interview, you can use these techniques to gain an unfair advantage over other job seekers. First, a word of caution. Do not go overboard and mirror 100% of every change in body position or gesture your interviewer makes. If you do, you will come across as extraordinarily awkward. The interviewer will pick up on it, and it will definitely make him or her uncomfortable. Maybe even uncomfortable enough not to hire you.

Remarkable Storytelling

The best interviewees are storytellers. If you haven't interviewed in a long while, then it is likely you are very rusty. You may even fall victim to the mistakes made by the majority of candidates: giving either short answers that don't give many details or going overboard and discussing non-relevant information. To fix this, you need to understand the components of a good story. There must be an interesting setting, sufficient edge of the seat action, a hero, a villain, and of course, an unexpected plot twist. In your interview preparation, you want to develop mini-stories of at least five professional accomplishments. These five accomplishments do not have to all be world-class amazing record setting awards. They can be, but most candidates can be successful with accomplishments such as meeting an extreme deadline or performance target, or receiving special customer service recognition. The main objective is that you want to have a sufficient database of stories that you can immediately refer to during the interview.

Advanced Note Taking

Job candidates miss the opportunity to take notes during the interview. In every interview, make sure you bring a compendium with a few resumes. Just showing up to the interview with your compendium shows that you are prepared and are taking the interview seriously. During the interview, you should only take brief notes and only when the interviewers are sharing very important information. This will show the interviewer you are very engaged.

Another benefit to taking notes is it allows you the chance to list out key words and industry jargon the interviewers are using which you can refer to later in your responses. This also helps if you may have multiple interviews on the same day. In these situations, you are going to have a challenging time developing remarkable follow-up questions and summaries of your interview if you did not take notes. Those candidates who took notes will have a distinct advantage to recall key information discussed during the interview to create outstanding thank you messages.

Ask for the Job

Many interviewees fail to implement a key negotiation strategy at the very end of their interview. Surprisingly and to their detriment, they never actually ask for the job. Do not make this common mistake. You should ask for the job even though it may not feel natural. You may not view yourself as a salesperson, and that is all right. Most professionals do not consider themselves to be good salesman. Unfortunately, you do need to implement some salesman tactics as you are selling YOU!

Chapter 8: What Not to Do in a Winning Interview

If you have not thought about common pitfalls to avoid during the job interview, then your preparation is incomplete.

Being Overconfident

There is a thin line between being confident about yourself and your skills and appearing overconfident. Employers like confidence but they abhor showing off unduly. Ensure that you avoid any kind of displays of ego or any outrageous claims. Confidence usually has a shade of humility to it.

Not Being Prepared

Today's interviewers are fairly ruthless against job applicants who come unprepared for the interview. The Internet is a veritable treasure house for all kinds of information and hence, hiding behind ignorance is not tolerated at all.

Being Disrespectful or Bad Behavior

You cannot be disrespectful to anybody on the panel no matter what personal prejudices you may have. It is critical that you make eye contact with the person who has asked a question while answering it instead of ignoring him or her and talking only to the seemingly most important individual on the panel.

Talking About Your Personal Life

There are times when it could be appropriate, but generally speaking, keep your personal life out of it. I have had interviewees discuss their parents' divorce, various childhood dramas, and bad breakups, amongst other topics. In most contexts, it's awkward. And again, don't give the interviewer the opportunity to think you're weird. Minimize your risk.

Over Sharing

It's important that you share the details of your professional – and personal, if asked – life, but it's equally as important not to over share. If you're asked a personal question, answer curtly, and don't delve into your family history and issues, because they're completely irrelevant. As for your past work experiences, don't share your entire history; just focus on the relevant parts, and those that would highlight the expertise employers would find useful to this particular position.

Losing Your Temper

Earlier, we mentioned the importance of not panicking when asked questions that make you feel a bit uncomfortable. It's also important to not lose your temper when faced with provocative questions. Sometimes, interviewers delve into topics that might be a bit sensitive for you or might hit a nerve. In cases like these, you need to maintain your composure and answer calmly, even if you feel strongly about something. Just state your opinion and don't get into a heated argument; instead, present your point of view such as it may be and don't fall into any traps that might be set by the interviewer.

Whether you're being asked questions related to gender, age, religion, marital status, or whatever, don't get angry and offend the interviewer. If you feel that you can't do as mentioned above and answer calmly, then answer with a question about how this is relevant to the interview, or find a way to avoid answering the question politely. The important thing is never to lose it and start getting into a war of words that will lead nowhere.

Another technique some interviewers use is to try to blame you for a previous problem in a past job. In this case, you definitely need to control your temper and own up to the problem if it truly was your doing, or clarify things and explain exactly how things went down and how the situation is not as they understood it. These tactics are pretty common in interviews, and the aim is to test your limits and help employers determine whether or not you're a ticking time-bomb.

Avoid Saying "UHM", "UHH", "LIKE".

No one wants to hear a sentence full of uhmms because saying these words will make you sound uncertain of your answers. Eliminate these words as much as possible in your vocabulary.

Smoking or Drinking Before an Interview

It might seem a little obvious, but people are usually very nervous before interviews, and they sometimes need something to take the edge off. Well, use a stress ball or chew gum. Walking into an interview smelling like alcohol or cigarettes is one of the worst things you could do. It's not only upsetting to those around you because of the odor, but it also shows a lack of commitment and respect to the entire process. Not to mention, you can be seriously offending the person interviewing you.

Using Excessive Hand Motions

Keep your hands within your shoulders, either on the table or on your lap. Feel free to use small hand motions, but keep it to just that. If the interviewer starts noticing your hands, reduce your hand motions immediately.

Don't Ask Them for Feedback

One of the mistakes a lot of people do is ask for feedback towards the end of the interview, and it's not a very wise thing to do. Asking questions like, "Is there anything you think I should work on?" or "According to how the interview went, do you think there's a reason why you wouldn't consider me for this job?" is a very bad omen and it reflects insecurity and a severe lack of confidence. Not to mention the fact that you'd be putting your interviewers on the spot and making the situation needlessly awkward. The interviewers need time to assess your answers and the overall interview, and asking them questions like that would make the situation tense when it doesn't need to be. Also, when you ask questions like these, you're actually making them think of your shortcomings, which might've easily slipped their minds because you did well throughout the interview, for instance. When you ask them what you did wrong, they'll start recalling the answers that made them uneasy, which is definitely not good for your chances.

Keep it professional and try to be eloquent. Tell them to reach out and call you if they have any more questions or concerns they'd like to address. That way, you leave the door open for them to call you back, and you come off sounding confident and relaxed.

Badmouthing Previous Companies

It does not reflect well on you to talk negatively about companies on your resume. It's natural to have a few bad experiences, but be sure to paint them in the right light. If you talk negatively about a previous company, it implies that you will talk negatively about the company you're interviewing for now in the future. Organizations like to hire people who are problem solvers and can overcome difficult situations. They do not wish to hire people who cannot get along with others or have a habit of blaming others for their shortcomings. So if you criticize your previous supervisors or employers, you may not be hired. Remain as positive as possible even if your previous employer was unpleasant.

Following Up Post Interview With Answers to Questions You Got Wrong

If you think you answered a question incorrectly, do not follow up with an answer. Nothing good ever comes from that approach. If you feel that one question was the determining factor in your candidacy, you're wrong. And if you think that answering that question after the fact will help you, you are dead wrong. Swallow your pride, wait to hear back, and then learn from your mistakes using the growth mindset.

Appearing Arrogant

There's a fine line between boasting about your accomplishments and appearing arrogant. Always credit your team and your colleagues for success while focusing on how your accomplishments improved the company's top and bottom lines. No one owes you a job; you have to earn the opportunity. If you really are the right candidate for the job, your credentials and professionalism will speak for itself. You appear full of yourself if you make inflated claims about your qualifications, bad mouth previous employers or make assumptions about the job role.

Lack of Communication

Prepare questions that the interviewer might ask you and make sure to practice how to answer them. Another red flag for them is when you are looking at your watch so often because this shows lack of interest in your conversation with the interviewer and it makes them feel you want to end it as soon as possible.

Poor Manners

Lack of business etiquette will tell a lot about you. It will make the interviewer see you as a future employee that is hard to work with, showing no concern of the people you interact with, and worse, you might look rude to them. Work on how you behave and your body language.

Never Swear

Even if the interviewer does it, you can never swear in an interview. It's pretty normal to do it in everyday life and in social settings, and it might even be acceptable in the workplace itself. But when you're on the spot to get the job, swearing is pretty inappropriate, not to mention unprofessional.

Never Look at Your Watch

This one is pretty self-explanatory. No matter how long the interview takes and how exhausted you feel, you can never look at your watch. It's impolite, unprofessional, and just plain out wrong. Go with the flow, and you can check the time after the interview is done. Besides, you're here to land the opportunity of the lifetime – do you really have somewhere better to be?

Lack of Commitment

Do not bring up stories that will make them feel that you are not going to stay with them for a long time. Some people apply for jobs only to use them as stepping stones in order to reach their real target job. So assure them that it is your top choice to apply for. This will relieve them of that suspicion. Prove to them how concerned you are of the company's welfare and how you will prioritize it as long as you are working for them.

Bringing Up Money Talk Too Early

We all agree that money is a major factor in deciding what job we want to apply for but bringing up questions on salary too early will make you look like you're just after the money. As much as possible, wait for them to tell you about it before trying to ask questions regarding pay. If they are considering hiring you, sooner or later they will discuss this topic with you and that's when you start negotiating with them.

Inflating Your Expertise by Lying

Yes, you are proud of what you have achieved until now, but you cannot expect yourself to know everything. It is perfectly alright to accept not knowing an answer to a question that has been asked. You could look at ways to better understand the question by reframing it or asking for more clarification before you answer it. Also by asking questions, you're showing a sense of eagerness and inquisitiveness that though you do not have the answer right now, you are interested enough in answer the questions as best you can.

However, it is unforgivable if you chose to make up answers to inflate your expertise. Do not try to guess the answers. An efficient interviewer will catch it immediately and that can spell disaster for you. Instead, simply state that you do not know! This forthrightness is appreciated by most interviewers and is definitely a better option than making up answers.

Apologizing Unduly

It is a courteous thing to apologize for a mistake. However, interviewers do not appreciate undue apologies. Saying sorry needlessly reflects an irritating lack of confidence. Moreover, apologizing often could also present you as a very weak personality and no company wants to hire a weak person. For example, instead of saying, "sorry", say "yes, but however.." or "well it seems.."

Complaining About Your Present Job

Do NOT EVER do this! Do not present your current employer in the wrong light. Do not talk about how difficult it is to work for your current boss. Do not complain about your present working environment. No one wants to recruit a complaining person! Moreover, your potential employer must not get the impression that you are running from somewhere. It is far better that the interviewer thinks that you see the job as being advancement, rather than an escape route.

Giving Practiced Answers

Yes, you need to practice your answers. But the practice should be so good that it sounds very natural to the interviewers. A "rehearsed" answer is frowned upon by most interviewers. In fact, good interviewers can catch answers that have been picked up from guidebooks. So, prepare your answers to back up your personality and experience. This will ensure that your answers do not sound practiced or rehearsed.

Dressing Sloppily

While you do not have to dress like a model or a film star, it is imperative that you present a clean, groomed look. Unkempt hair, clothes that are torn or not ironed, dirty shoes and socks that look ridiculous are an immediate put-off. Please prepare well, wear a good set of clean clothes, and appear neat and tidy at the interview.

Furthermore, wear a dress shirt and dress pants/skirt. Block out as many piercings and tattoos as much as possible. Yes, we all have our own individuality, but some employers are still old fashioned and like the clean look. Just present yourself as best as you can and because first impressions are important! Many people know that dressing appropriately is an important part of an interview, but some do not know what "appropriately" means. You need to dress to impress and avoid loud, colorful or tasteless clothing. There is an array of things to avoid like: strong perfume or cologne, nail polish that draws attention, too much jewelry, obvious tattoos, men with piercings visible, etc.

You want the interview to be focused on you, not what you are wearing. Many judgments can be made based on what you are wearing and how you present yourself. If done well, you make a great impression. If done poorly, you will be talked about and not in a good way.

Pointing

During the interview, the recruiter sets a distance between him and the applicant. This is to keep things professional. Although not obviously, pointing your finger at the person you are talking to breaks that space. The act in itself is accusatory and blaming, so avoid doing this during the interview.

Crossing the Arms Over the Chest

Crossing your arms over your chest is a very defensive gesture. It's as if you do not want the interviewer to know anything about you, which cannot be because the purpose of the interview is to let them know how you can contribute to their company. On top of that, this gesture will make the recruiter feel like you are overriding his authority, as if whatever you say is right and you do not care what he thinks about it.

Fidgeting

Fidgeting is a very distracting body language and it delivers the message that you are not confident. Examples of fidgeting are nail biting, wringing your hands, continuously tapping your feet, and playing with the seams of your suit.

One of the worst body movements you can do is excessive fidgeting. It makes you look like you can't wait to get out of there, and you come off as scared and extremely nervous. So, stay calm and quiet in your chair, and for the love of all that it is holy, don't shake your legs! Even if they're underneath a table, the interviewer will feel like there's an earthquake going on! The best you can do with your feet is to keep them firmly on the ground, and it'll even help you focus on answering the more difficult questions.

When you are talking, the goal is to make the interviewer see your point. He won't be able to concentrate if you are fidgeting will catch his attention.

Nodding Too Much

Nodding too much is a common mistake among applicants. In their desire to let the interviewer know that they are listening and that they understand, they always nod. The problem here is it distracts the interviewer and instead of thinking that you indeed comprehend what he is telling you, he will think of the opposite: you don't really understand that's why you keep on nodding!

Hands Behind the Back or Inside the Pockets

Like crossing the arms, hands in the pocket or at your back means that you are unwilling to be approached. Most applicants do this to prevent themselves from fidgeting; but still, this is a major body language red flag. The interviewer will feel like you are holding back and your lack of comfort will dominate the whole interview.

Staring

Because you do not want to break the eye contact, you opt for staring too much! Don't do that, for one thing, that's a creepy gesture and second, it will look like you are the one who is scrutinizing the interviewer. Just be natural and don't forget to blink.

Mismatched Facial Expression

Sometimes, what your voice implies seem different from what your expression shows. Doing this (even though most of the time it is unintentional) will make the recruiter think that you are pretentious. Don't be too caught up on the rule that you have to smile. If what you are talking about is a serious discussion, opt for a serious expression and soften it if the conversation shifts to a more pleasant track.

While some of the mistakes mentioned above may seem terribly basic, you would be surprised to know how many job seekers repeatedly make them unwittingly. Make sure these mistakes are deeply etched in your mind so that the avoidance of them becomes a habit rather than a conscious effort.

Arriving Late

It goes without saying; you never want to be late for an interview. It is one of the biggest deal breakers if you cannot keep time on the first day. If you are not five minutes early, then you are late. It is recommended that you arrive early and get accustomed to the organization's ambiance. If you are uncontrollably running late, make sure to call and inform them of your delay. Always have the contact information of the person organizing your visit for such a reason, but make sure to overcome all obstacles to arrive at the scheduled time. It shows that you are punctual and you can be trusted with routines or to hit deadlines, or even to save time for the company. Conversely, arriving too early gives employers the first reason to start judging you from a negative light.

Unprepared for Questions

You want to sell the idea that you are the perfect candidate for the job. You cannot do that by stumbling all over your words and questions. You need to be prepared for what might be asked of you and know how to form an intelligent, articulate answer to that question.

Prepare and practice is the best method to successful answers. Think through what you might want to know about a candidate and answer those questions. Give solid, positive answers and make sure you make the interviewer see that you are the best candidate.

Salary Focus

Money is something you stay away from until the interviewer brings it up. If you are too focused on salary or benefits, you are telling your interviewer that the job means nothing to you and you are after a pay check. You should never ask questions like, "what is my salary?" "How soon will I be promoted?" "How soon can I take vacation?"

These are all things that indicate you are not serious about your career or the job. By having an employee that is self-centered and focused on the perks, the company will not gain anything. You will not be able to sell yourself as a candidate if these types of questions are asked.

Improper Documentation

Just because you have been called does not mean that the person interviewing you received the actual resume. Make sure you have the documents you need to be prepared. Bring extra resumes and reference lists. You cannot be too prepared. Assume that the person you are meeting has nothing to work with.

Perhaps you are meeting with a panel and did not know it. You should have several copies of your resume so you have the ability to show that you are prepared. This will make a huge impression and work well in your favor.

Dishonesty and Rudeness

Attitude has a lot to do with who is hired and who is not. Do not lie. With modern technology, many things can be verified and lying in the interview or on your resume will be found out. Once you have been caught lying, the game is over. You have ruined your chances permanently with that company.

Get Caught Lying

A definite guarantee that you will not get the job is to lie during the job interview. If you are going to make a bold claim or state something that is not true, seriously think about your chances of getting away with it. Companies run background checks on potential hires. Whether it is about your credentials, accomplishments or your work history, honesty will usually be the best policy.

Inappropriate Humor

Be confident, but avoid cracking jokes unnecessarily or saying things probably best left unsaid. A little touch of humor could work in your favor, provided that it is appropriate to the context of the interview. You do not need to be funny, especially when it is at the expense of appropriateness and formality. The last thing you want is for the hiring manager to think you are not serious about the job opportunity.

Getting Personal

A job interview is a formal meeting to assess if you are the right fit for a job. Everything in your personal life, your subjective opinions and how you are feeling should be left outside the door, and not be brought up during the interview.

Ask When the Interview Will End

You will also be doing just as much damage by constantly looking at your watch. When you are called in for a job interview, you are expected to make time for it, if you really want to get the job.

Chapter 9: Tips and Tricks

Research About the Organization and Interviewers

The interview will be smoother if you know the key information about the company. Refer to the organization's website, latest press releases, and social media articles to gain an insight into the company's goals.

Read the Job Description Carefully

You can print out the description of the job and read through it thoroughly. Underline the specific skills the employer is looking for in a candidate. Think about some things from your previous and current jobs that align with the job requirements. Try to come up with concrete examples to use in the interview.

Use the STAR Method for Answering Questions

You will almost certainly be asked to describe a previous experience where you used a specific skill, so you should be prepared to tell stories of your past work experience. Follow the STAR technique where you first describe the situation, then the task, the action you took, and the final result.

Use the Help of a Friend

Practicing is most effective when you say the answers out loud. You can either say them in front of a mirror or ask a friend to help you with the answers. In this way, you will gain confidence and be well prepared for the interview. If you do enlist the help of a friend, show them the job description and help them brainstorm potential questions for you to practice answering.

Prepare a Reference List

You may be asked to give some references prior to or after the interview. If your reference list is ready beforehand, the hiring process may move more quickly. Be sure to contact your references before submitting your list to the employer. Make sure they are willing to be a reference for you.

Keep Examples of Work Ready

You will probably be asked to show some past work you have done that is related to this job. After you have reviewed the job description, think about the work you have done in clubs, volunteer positions, or past jobs that shows you are prepared for and have the experience necessary to be successful at the job.

Be Ready to Ask Smart Questions

Interviews involve a conversation between the interviewers and the interviewee, so you are expected to ask some pertinent questions to show your genuine interest in the organization and position. Be prepared to ask some smart questions to show off your skills and impress your employers.

Plan Your Attire Beforehand

If possible, find out about the company's dress code for the workplace and dress accordingly. You can try to talk to someone who works there, or you can do some research to find an appropriate outfit. It is better to be overdressed than underdressed. Prepare your outfit the night before so you do not have to worry about clothes on the day of your interview.

Use Ms. or Mr. When Addressing Your Interviewers

Have you ever noticed that most people prefer to be called by their first name? When last did you hear someone instruct you to refer to him or her with his or her last name? The main reason for this is that using the last name when addressing someone is a show of respect. In a world where little of this is going around, you are more likely to stand out from the crowd. NB: throughout your interview, the interviewer will be trying to assess how easy it will be to manage and work with you. As much as employers are looking for leaders and self starters, sometimes they need someone who can do his/her job and act like a soldier.

Look People in The Eye

As a point of emphasis, body language is very important when it comes to displaying appropriate interview etiquette. Studies have shown that about 80 percent of our conversations are non-verbal. One good way to build trust and connect with people is to look them in the eyes. This also applies when you find yourself in a group interview. Most people tend to show nervousness when under pressure, lack confidence and don't usually smile. Something as simple as a friendly smile can make the world of difference in showcasing leadership and confidence, even if you are a nervous wreck.

Let the Interviewer Lead the Interview

If your interviewer appears to be somehow laid back or soft spoken, you may feel the urge to get things moving by trying to take back some control. Before you know it, you are rambling.

Overcome this temptation and let the hiring manager run the show. If you experience moments of silence, just embrace the silence. If you are adequately prepared for the interview, then you have nothing to worry about. Talking too much is one of the most common mistakes people get wrong during interviews.

Sit Up and Lean Slightly Forward

Even if you have the excellent qualifications, you stand a very big chance of being rejected just for being too laid back in the interview, I mean literally. This is one of the most common reasons older candidates are often prejudged as lacking in ambition and drive. However, you also need to be on your guard even if you are a younger job seeker to avoid coming out too relaxed or casual.

Things to Take to the Interview

You should take a minimum of five printed copies of your resume if there are multiple interviewers. You can highlight some specific accomplishments in your personal copy so that you may refer to it and discuss it during the interview.

Take a notebook and pen to jot down points during the interview. These will be useful during the follow-up process.

Arrive Early

Plan your schedule so that you arrive at least ten to fifteen minutes early. If you are using public transportation, have a backup plan in case there are sudden closures or delays.

Make a Fantastic First Impression

Be careful about the little things. See to it that your shoes are shining, there are no holes or stains on your clothes, and your nails are not dirty. Dress appropriately and try to look professional. Keep a smile on your face and exhibit confidence by standing tall.

Behave in a Courteous Manner

Treat everyone with respect including the people you meet in the parking lot, at the security station, and at the front desk. The potential employer may ask them for feedback about you.

Display Positive Body Language

Walk and sit in a confident manner and keep your back straight. You can manage your anxiety and nervousness by breathing deeply and exhaling slowly. Shake hands with the interviewer and smile.

Remember the Four C's for Communication.

Clear: Ensure that the statements you make are clear. It should not be possible to interpret them in various ways.

Concise: You should be brief. You need not elaborate on things and give countless details unless it is necessary or you have been asked to do so.

Coherent: See to it that there is a flow to your statements. They should be connected in a coherent manner.

Complete: You should tell the complete story without leaving out the essential bits of information.

Be Authentic and Positive

You can win over the employers by being sincere and genuine during the conversation. Displaying positivity with good body language and a smile can help keep the interview flowing in a constructive and light direction.

Be honest about your accomplishments and skills. Do not exaggerate them, but do not undersell yourself. Focus on the key strengths you have that make you the right fit for the job. Explain the way that the strengths are related to the goal of the company or department and how they may be beneficial for the employer.

Support Your Answers with Examples

Give examples from your previous jobs where you successfully performed tasks related to this job description. Include concrete and quantifiable data to demonstrate your specific accomplishments.

Give Concise and Pertinent Answers

Do not waste time rambling. This is why it is important to practice your answers so that you can respond in an appropriate and relevant manner without taking too much time for each answer. Unless you are asked for a detailed answer, spend only two or three minutes on each answer.

Ask About the Subsequent Steps

You may ask the interviewer, recruiter, or hiring manager what you are expected to do after the interview. You may have to provide a reference list, write some assignment, or appear for another interview.

Send a Thank You Note

You can send letters or emails to each of the interviewers to thank them individually. You can use the notes taken in the course of the interview and create distinct emails for each interviewer.

Get Feedback

Many organizations provide feedback about your performance during the interview and at the assessment centers. In case the facility is not available in the company you have interviewed with, you can ask for feedback directly from them.

After getting the feedback, you should critically review all of the things about your interview. By doing so, you can learn from experience and also be better prepared for future occasions. Ask yourself how you think you did and make notes to review your performance.

Don't Leave Home without These

Do not face the hiring manager without bringing these job interview essentials. Never forget to bring your resume. Do not assume that just because you e-mailed or sent them a copy already, that your interviewer would obviously have a copy printed out already. Print out more than enough copies for the number of interviewers you have as well as for yourself.

Make sure that the printouts are clear and the papers are not folded or creased when you hand them out. You should also print out as many copies of your cover letter to go with your resume. Also, have on hand a list of your references including their names, positions and contact details.

Confirm

Keep in mind to call the office of the hiring manager the day before your scheduled interview. This is common courtesy and shows that you are organized and respectful of your appointments. It also allows you to truly confirm your schedule and make any adjustments in advance should any problems arise. It is possible that your interview schedule may have been overlooked by a secretary or the date is incorrect due to a typo error in an e-mail sent to you.

Brand Yourself

Here's a question: What's the first thing that comes to mind when you think of companies like Apple or BMW? There are certain qualities that we attribute to brands all over the world, and our favorite ones are associated with certain images and notions. Well, you too are a brand, and you need the interviewers to walk out of the interview with a strong impression about one or two of your qualities that will stick with them. So, focus and try to find your most important qualities – that should be related to your compatibility with the job – and try to infuse them into your answers and how you approach questions. This is your personal brand, and if it's good enough and you're able to sell it well enough, the job is yours.

Jack of All Trades, Master of None

Never portray yourself as one. 'Jack of all trades, master of none' is an expression that refers to those who have explored many avenues and gained a lot of experiences in various fields, but have mastered none. You don't want that attribute. Yes, it's important to have different skills that would help you in different situations, but you need to portray yourself as a specialist, a person who has a particular set of skills or experience in a specific field.

When you highlight your skills and qualifications in light of a certain area or two, you're showing the interviewers that you can maintain your focus and grow in a certain direction, and more importantly, you're the guy to handle those specific areas of the job. Maybe you're great at cutting costs, and you've helped do so in all your previous jobs. Or you're great in developing successful teams working under you, and you've helped a lot of people grow and develop. Whatever it is, when you shed light on that particular quality, you're giving the interviewers a direction in which they could use you, thus increasing your chances of getting hired.

Maintain the Balance Between Professional and Fun

We've discussed the importance of being a professional and maintaining a certain discipline during the interview, as well as not appearing too casual and relaxed. It's also important to not appear too rigid and formal because the work environment might actually be fun. So, as with all else pertaining to your interview, you need to find a balance between both. This is not just in regards to your appearance and how you speak or what you say, but it's also about how you approach problems and situations you might face in the future.

You want to walk away from the interview having left the impression that you're a reliable and trust-worthy person who will handle work and all things related in the utmost professionalism, which will reflect positively on both you and the company.

Don't Bc Too Vague

No interviewer likes to hear general, fluffy statements that might be nonsense for all they know. Generalizations portray image inexperience, of a person who doesn't know what they're talking about, and they give a pretty bad impression about you. So, as specific as possible. Use relevant examples and situations, and explain what you would do in each. Don't say things like, "Generally, the best course of action would be to...." Instead say something like, "If this situation happens, I will do the following..." Being specific is always better than being vague, and blanket statements won't get you very far.

Own Up to Your Mistakes

Everybody makes mistakes, and it's a natural part of any job. Sometimes you will be asked about a situation where you failed at a job or a task you were given. It's very important that you be honest when telling these stories and own up to your mistakes. Don't try to shift the blame and claim it was your colleagues' fault, that you did your job right and they were the reason why things went awry.

One of the most important qualities of a leader is taking responsibility for your actions and owning up to your mistakes, and that is something you're going to have to do. If you were in the wrong, admit it and explain what steps you took to make amends. That is much better than claiming you did everything right, and the project went south because of someone else's mistakes.

Be Honest

Do not lie to the interviewer. In this digital age, information is readily and easily accessible to anyone who needs it. Be careful with the data you put on your resume for these can be verified through different sources.

Turn Off Your Cellphone

It is common knowledge that it would indeed be very be rude to take a call, or even read an SMS or e-mail during a job interview. Just turn off that thing! If you cannot afford to do so, then switch it to silent mode. Turn off any alarms you have set on your phone, too. Your phone ringing could possibly disrupt your conversation with the hiring manager and disturb an interview that is actually going pretty well.

Listen: Be polite and Mind Your Manners

Listen first to what your interviewer has to say before you go ahead and speak. Do not talk over him or interrupt him when speaking.

Do Not Talk Too Much

Applicants who rambled on and on about a particular topic might turn off job interviewers. Notice when you are already repeating yourself or talking in a loop or taking a pretty long time to answer a simple question. This usually shows that you do not know the answer to a question and the words coming out of your mouth are empty. Sometimes, it might be due to nervousness caused by the interview itself or perhaps the lie that you are telling. So compose yourself before continuing to answer a question.

Arrive Early

Punctuality is key. At any cost, do not be tardy. It is a sign that you are unreliable and unprofessional.

Plan your schedule so that you arrive at least ten to fifteen minutes early. If you are using public transportation, have a backup plan in case there are sudden closures or delays.

Avoid Swearing

Unless a ceiling panel falls on your head and you need to be rushed to the hospital because of the gash, there is pretty much no excuse for using any expletives during your interview. Even if you're relating a true story, omit the curse words.

Avoid Sexist and Racist Language

In fact, avoid any language or terms that could potentially offend anyone. You have no idea how people feel about any of those things, whether or not they have friends or spouses of one persuasion or another, or pretty much anything at all. If you offend someone in your interview you can kiss the job goodbye.

Avoid Personal Details

Employment law states that you cannot be asked if you're married, how many children you have, if you care for elderly parents or a disabled family member, or pretty much anything having to do with your personal life.

Chapter 10: Warnings

Don't try too hard to make the interviewer like you. They may interpret this unfavorably, either deciding that you are desperate to find a job, or that you are somewhat disingenuous. Try just to be calm, confident and professional.

Always try to emit a positive attitude and a feeling of wellbeing throughout the interview process, even if your expression is serious and you don't often smile. Even if you are tired, the feeling of inner happiness will make your eyes shine, which will be received positively by any interviewer.

Always remember that during the interview, the person interviewing you will not only be considering what he or she thinks of you, but will also be considering you from the point of view of their clients. This is especially true if the majority of your duties will involve direct communication with clients. Also, they will be thinking how other employees of the company, whom you will have to work with, will view you. Your suitability will not only depend on how well you can perform your tasks, but also how well you work in a team environment. Therefore, sometimes it helps when answering questions to imagine that you are talking to a client or a colleague. Generally speaking, you should appear more serious if you are talking about your duties or products that you worked on and speak in a friendly and slightly more relaxed manner if you are talking about your personal life or relationships with colleagues.

The best emotion that you can convey at all times is calmness. Only in that state are we capable of thinking clearly and quickly. Also, you will make a much better impression if you talk to the interviewer calmly and patiently.

Until the very last second, you should keep your back straight, shoulders relaxed, smile, and move calmly and confidently.

Some people have a bad habit of interrupting someone else when speaking. This very annoying habit shows lack of courtesy. Let the person interviewing you finish making their point and then add to the conversation or respond to their question.

Interviewers will often use a technique called "projection questions". You can be asked a question that initially seems not to apply to you directly. For example, "Describe the ideal relationship between colleagues" or "In which situations is it ok to lie?". Normally, when answering questions like these, people begin to unconsciously describe events that are based on their personal experience. Using this technique, the interviewer is trying to get as much additional information about you as possible. Be mindful of this tactic and remember to always answer questions from a positive angle.

If they mention that you are under qualified in some way, acknowledge any true statements and then pivot the conversation to a more positive stance. This is usually how you plan to correct the issue or move onto something that you consider to be equivalent experience.

As expected, an interviewer will ask the applicant questions during the interview process. However, the prepared and successful job seeker should also pose questions back to the prospective company.

This is a fantastic way to show the potential employer that you are an above average candidate. A lot of candidates do not ask employers very many questions and you will stand out from the crowd if you do. Asking detailed questions shows the employer that you are a candidate who is taking the opportunity seriously.

A master question list is a helpful way of ensuring that all of the important details are discussed when under the pressure of an interview. Maintaining these in a spreadsheet or a bulleted list of these questions is recommended to keep them all neatly organized in one location. You will have to choose which questions are applicable to each interview because each one is a unique experience.

Often people wonder exactly how they should act during an interview. Interviews are stressful and can bring out some bad habits in people but there are some things you can do to make sure that you are behaving appropriately during an interview. So much of the interview is based on how you behave. It is not all about what you say. Your personality can be a big factor in whether you get the job or not. There are some things to pay close attention to when you are interviewing.

Two things to never do are chew gum or mints and use slang in speech. It is unattractive, you cannot hide it and it is rude. Never have things in your mouth during an interview. Speak well and intelligently. You do not want to come off as unintelligent or unprofessional.

It is inevitable that you will find that interviews are one of the most stressful things you can go through in your life. We always look forward to getting a job but don't want to deal with the interview process. It is difficult and anxiety-inducing. Our stomach clenches as we prepare to go to the interview room. We may have shortness of breath and wheezing in our chests. Additionally, perhaps we will experience butterflies in our stomachs. It is always a challenge, because you can never be prepared enough for an interview. There will be unexpected turns that you have to try to get ready for, and sometimes, you just have to have the spontaneity to handle whatever the interviewer throws at you. That's where this chapter comes in handy. We're going to show you how to roll with the punches and other challenges you may face in an interview situation.

Conclusion

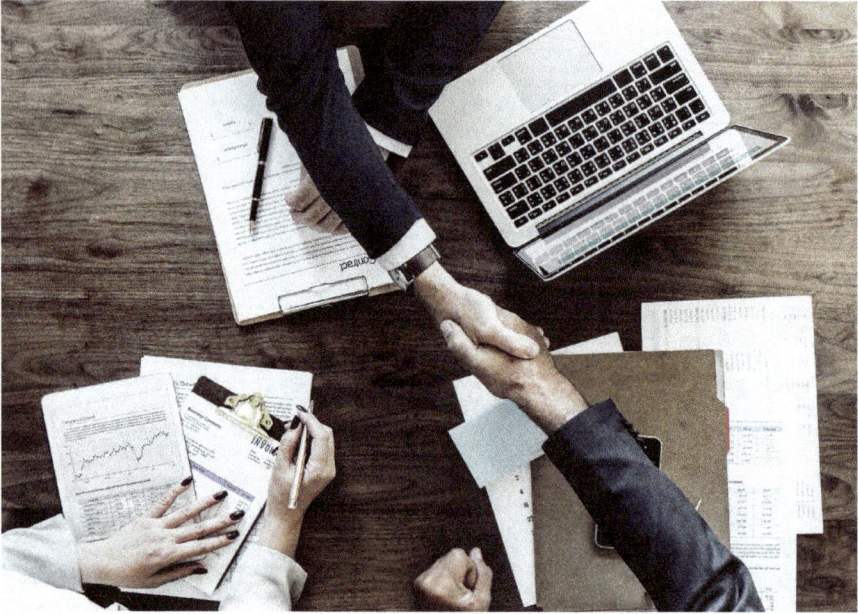

Thank you for making it through to the end of this book. I hope this book has helped you know what you can do and what you avoid in order to ace that interview. Now you can be sure that with the tips you have learnt here, you will never fail to pass an interview again.

To get ready for the interview, you will have to prepare yourself with a pep talk, freshen up, and smile to get the adrenaline going. Additionally, you need to push away from getting into panic mode. Try to calm yourself. Then, give yourself the biggest compliment that you can, to push you forward into the interview with the confidence that will land you the job. You can do it. Follow these tips, and you will feel much better when you get to the interview. We guarantee it!

It's necessary to conclude your job interview while leaving a favorable final impression, and that involves saying goodbye to the hiring manager properly and settling the business meeting in a way that will positively impact the future.

Final impressions can be the most enduring and they are just as important as the first impressions since people remember the beginning and the most.

The more you prepare, the more the chances of success. Fear is a highly debilitating emotion that prevents clear thinking. In a panic mode, even the simplest of questions will appear difficult and answers will evade you. So, do not panic.

CPSIA information can be obtained
at www.ICGtesting.com
Printed in the USA
BVHW012354170221
600363BV00005BA/222